30 Ballparks in 30 Days
A Journal from the Road

For the fans,

30 Ballparks in 30 Days
A Journal from the Road

By
Travis Greene

It was April 18, 2009, when we set out on our journey. Spring was fresh in the air and the baseball season was only a couple weeks old and still full of promise when we put our first (of what would become over 18,000) mile behind us.

At that time, we didn't know what would become of us. Was attempting to see all 30 Major League ballparks in 30 days while only driving ambitious? Or was it stupid?

We didn't know. But what we *did* know was that we were on the trip of a lifetime – four avid baseball fans on the open road to experience our national pastime against the backdrop of America and make a movie out of our adventures. Could it get any better than this? My three biggest passions in life are film, baseball and traveling, so this was like a dream.

Out of pure curiosity, I put up a poll online before we left to see if people thought we could do it or not. There were 846 unique votes; 147 were in our favor.

That number didn't deter us. If anything, it made us more determined, focused us, and helped us realize that we *could* do this and we *would* do it. We adopted the motto "whatever it takes."

It's important to point out that a baseball road trip is not an original idea. People do it all the time. Ours, however, was taken to the extreme and I think that's where this one is a little different. In every city we visited, we met fans who have dreamed about taking a road trip like this. We received emails and facebook messages from people all across the country sharing their baseball stories with us, whether it be ballpark trips that they had taken or fond memories from their past. People cherish their baseball memories.

Selfishly, on that April 18 in 2009, we set out in our Mini-Vanbino thinking that this trip was solely for us, ignorant to the fact that there were people out there who envied what we were doing. After an outpouring of support and interest from thousands of people across the country, we quickly realized that this road trip wasn't just for us anymore but for that whole community of "ballpark chasers" and baseball fans, who, we came to learn, weren't strangers at all.

The pages that follow are from the journal I kept during those 30 days of living on the road. I knew before we left that the Trip would be an epic one and I wanted to preserve every aspect of it as best I could. Although we had the cameras rolling for the documentary, tape can't capture feelings and emotions like the written word can and I didn't want any detail forgotten, any mile missed, or any sighting surrendered to bad memory. For me, this was a trip of a lifetime and one that can never be duplicated. I realized then as I realize now that by some miraculous twist of fate, I was lucky enough to have been granted the opportunity to take an adventure like this and I want to bring you along for the ride. In the beginning this journal was meant just for me, but now I'd like to share it with you.

I once heard a great quote about baseball - "the games are exciting and the moments they produce are memorable, but it's the life around baseball, it's people and personalities, that make it all so much fun." We learned this firsthand. What started out as a trip about baseball, ended up being a trip about the life *around* baseball and the people who make it all so much fun.

So this one's for you, the baseball fan and the ballpark junkie, who were all there with us in spirit. You helped us do this, and this adventure is as much yours as it is mine.

Travis Greene
Philadelphia, PA
April, 2012

The Team

The four of us met while working at a video production house in Center City Philadelphia. Sharing a common passion for baseball, we bonded quickly.

Travis, 25

Freelance video editor
Philadelphia, PA

Joey, 27

Freelance video editor
Philadelphia, PA

Pedro, 26

Freelance camera operator
Philadelphia, PA

Glenn, 42

Freelance video editor
Philadelphia, PA

The Vanbino, 1

2009 Toyota Sienna
Philadelphia, PA

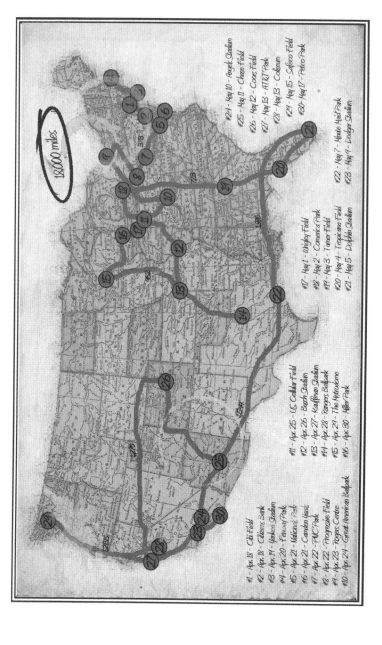

The Route

If our route looks chaotic, well, it's because it was. In order to see a game in every ballpark, the team had to obviously be playing at home, so we had to schedule our trip around only home games. There's no point showing up in Denver if the Rockies are playing in Phoenix, you know? The result was this ping-pong dash around the country.

The Rules

There were a couple rules we had to follow on this ballpark trip –

1. In order to make a stop official, we had to be inside the ballpark while a game was being played. Because we were on such a rigid day-to-day schedule, any rainouts or even rain delays could spell disaster – it would be nearly impossible to return to a city within our 30-day timeframe.

2. We had to drive the whole way, to every city, to every stop on our route. Taking a train or a plane at any point was forbidden.

Well, if this is any indication of how the Trip is going to go, we're in a lot of trouble. The lady at the front desk told us that Rickwood was just a 10-minute drive from the hotel, but here we are, 30 minutes later, and more lost than ever. We knew we were in trouble when our Garmin led us to a dead-end and said in its electronic female voice, "You have reached your destination."

"No we haven't," I thought as I stared at the barren parking lot of an old abandoned factory that sat in front of us.

I knew, also, that we were in trouble when I turned onto 6th Avenue North that branched off of 6th *Street* North... and we had just come from 6th *Court SW*, two blocks down the road. At this point, I wouldn't be surprised if we come to the intersection of 1st Avenue and 1st Avenue... the "nexus of the universe," as Joey called it.

"Dude, we're going in circles," Joey said from the passenger seat. "That's the same car wash we've passed twice... we're going in circles."

"Ask this guy." I pull alongside a Humpdee-Dumpdee looking fellow walking down the street. He's in uniform but he's not a police officer... and he's not military, either. Park ranger perhaps? But he's not wearing one of those ranger hats...

"Excuse me, sir!" Joey calls to him. The middle-aged man turns to us, his wild, thin, white hair dancing in the breeze and his jolly, puffy cheeks as red as a tomato. His forehead was glistening in sweat and when I saw his face, he reminded me of a mix between Santa Claus and Curly Howard. "We're trying to get to Rickwood?"

"The ball field?" he shouts back from the sidewalk. His voice is high-pitched and squeaky almost, not at all the deep baritone I was expecting to come from his enormous torso.

"Yeah, Rickwood Field," Joey answered. Curly waddled up to our car like a penguin from the water and leaned against it. He hunched forward and as his giant head came further and further into our car, Joey had to recline in his seat as far as possible to avoid any kind of body-to-body contact. He was invading Joey's personal bubble and if Joey hadn't reclined in his seat, they'd be touching cheeks right now.

"You fellas ain't from Birminham," he said in a thick Southern draw.

"No, sir. Philadelphia," I said. I glanced at Joey and I could see how uncomfortable he was. Not only was Curly's head literally inside our car, but his arm was, as well. The man was clueless.

"Well, let's see..." he said looking up through the windshield. A long moment of silence passed. Then he turned his head and looked through the back window. He breathed heavily. "Let's see here... Rickwood, huh?"

I noticed a big bead of sweat form at the rim of his hair as he thought.

"I'm trying to think of the easiest way for you fellas."

"That would be great," I said. "Even our GPS got lost!" I couldn't take my eyes off that bead of sweat. With his head still over Joey's lap and less than a foot from his face, I hoped – prayed even – for Joey's sake, that that bead decided to roll down the other side because if not - kerplunk! Right on Joey's lap. It wasn't looking good, though. I could see that Joey saw it, too, but I think he was more concerned with the wheezy, hot breathing in his face.

"Yep, well, that'll happen. Ever since they ran that damned interstate through here nobody knows where to go." He finally pulled his head out and the bead of sweat dripped onto the window frame of the van.

Joey glanced over at me in wide-eyed horror. Then the man looked to the sky.

"Yea-up, it's fixin' to rain alright," he said getting distracted.

The weather this morning said there was only a 20% chance of rain but the skies did look threatening.

"You're close," Curly said. "You're gonna wanna turn around. Stay on this road until you see the train tracks then take the first right. Go down that road, I can't think of the name, but go down that road, around the bend, and then Rickwood will be at the end of that road... should be at the end of the road," and with that he let out a deep, breathy, belly laugh.

Curly slapped the side of my car like it was a horse and we took off for the train tracks.

"I thought he was gonna crawl right in," Joey said as we turned around. "I thought he was going to crawl right in and sit on my lap."

Sure enough, past the train tracks and around the bend, Rickwood Field sat at the end of the road. Curly had come through.

Standing outside in the gravel parking lot, Rickwood doesn't look like anything special. It's short – just two stories high, if that – and small, its stucco walls painted a dark green color that seems to be fading under the intense Alabama sun. On the front above the entrance between two roof awnings with terra cotta shingles is the name "RICKWOOD."

Nothing special. Plain, even; a building I'm sure I would have driven right past without even noticing it. But looks can be deceiving because inside these green, stucco walls is a history as rich as they come. This is the oldest ballpark in America, but its true distinction comes through the greats it has seen play here.

Rickwood is, and always has been, a melting pot for baseball. Not only has it played host to the white greats of the Major Leagues, but it has played host to black greats of the Negro Leagues in a time when baseball was still segregated – Babe Ruth and Josh Gibson, Ted Williams and Cool Papa Bell, Satchel Paige and Burleigh Grimes all shared the same bench, the same mound, the same plate.

Yes, inside these green and white cement walls is where magic lives.

A light rain began to fall as we walked through an old wooden gate that sits crooked on its hinges. On it, hand-painted in big white letters – "NO BETTING IN THIS PARK." So cool... so old-fashioned. Even the advertising signs painted on the outfield wall are all in the style of 1920 ad campaigns. This park opened in 1910, two years before Fenway opened (the oldest park in the Majors) and they've done an amazing job preserving the nostalgic charm here. It's almost as if it's been left untouched for decades, forgotten by time, and stepping inside is like stepping back into a different era. I wouldn't be surprised if we saw Ty Cobb in the batter's box.

We walked out to the bleachers and sat in the cold, damp seats just behind the visitor's dugout. I looked out over the field... the perfectly manicured, immaculate, handsome field, its plush green grass like a velvet carpet draped over the land. Long ago when I first started really getting into the history of baseball, I read a quote from the MLB's seventh commissioner A. Bartlett Giamatti that has stuck with me – Giamatti liked to compare the ballpark to the idea of paradise and he found joy in explaining to people that, "the word 'paradise' was an ancient Persian word and its literal meaning is 'an enclosed green space'."

I like that. I think about it often (especially when I'm here at the ballpark) and how appropriate that definition is.

The rain got heavier. The white chalk along the foul lines began to bleed into the dirt like mascara around tearing eyes. Puddles were turning to pools and home plate was completely submerged in water.

"Those weathermen are snakes," Joey said. "20% chance my ass. Filthy snakes they are."

We didn't come to Rickwood to see a game today but it didn't matter - we were rained out anyway. So far, between getting lost and the weather, this day had been a disaster and I sat there, hoping, praying that this was not a sign of things to come. In two weeks we'd be embarking on the adventure of a lifetime and if this was a day on our Trip, we would have failed... it would have ended right here. Attempting 30in30 in April is risky but after months of working out a schedule, it was the only time, that *I* could find, 30in30 by only driving to be possible. There's a thin line between ambition and stupidity and right now I wasn't quite sure which side we were leaning on.

What's that quote, though? "You can't steal second with your foot on first?"

That sounds about right.

Saturday, April 18 — DAY 1
Doubleheader Day # 1 — New York and Philly
1:35 Game @ Citi Field (Ballpark #1)
7:35 Game @ Citizens Bank Park (Ballpark #2)
Total Miles Today — 330
Total Miles So Far — 0

11:30am

It's an easy drive from Philly to New York – you just jump on the Jersey Turnpike and in an hour-thirty, you're in Manhattan. We're lucky that our first drive of the Trip is an easy one but the first day of the Trip? Well, that's a different story. We have two games today (our first of five doubleheader days) and, by days end, we will have driven on this same 100 mile stretch of road through the heart of New Jersey not once but three times.

I watched the trees outside my window zip by as our speedometer touched 70. The hula girl on our dashboard danced to the bumps in the road.

"She's hot," Joey said with a devilish little smirk on one side of his mouth. "If she was real, she'd be hot... oh, by the way, I locked myself out last night."

Here we go. Joey is one of the funniest guys I know and his stories rarely disappoint. He has the gift of gab and is famous among friends for the witty remarks and clever catchphrases he coins. Joey grew up in a really small rural town outside the Poconos called Tannersville. In his 27 years, he hasn't gotten too far from home so, although he's looking forward to the ballparks, getting out and seeing the country is what he's really excited for.

"But luckily there's a narrow little alley right behind my apartment," he continued, "so, it was like 3am and I'm back there with all the cats and coons and everything and I have to Spiderman my way up the walls, right? Cause I'm on the third floor so I literally have one foot on my building and the other foot on the building behind me and I walk up the walls like I'm Jean Claude van Damme or something."

If I didn't know him then I would think he was exaggerating.

"So I get to the top and I'm stuck. I'm stuck. Three stories above the ground, straddling the alley and I'm stuck. My window is right there but I have no way of maneuvering over to it because my feet are holding me up. So there's a power line, right? I jump and grab onto the power line and swing to my window like I'm Tarzan. It was amazing! But nobody was there to witness it. No one will ever believe me."

"I don't believe you," I tell him.

"Wait, the power line?!" Glenn asks.

"The power line," Joey confirms. Glenn still looks at him disbelieving that he could survive a Tarzan swing from an electrical power line three stories above the ground. "I had rubber soles on…" Joey said as if it was obvious how it was possible.

"I don't get it," Glenn says and he sits back in his seat.

" I know. No one will ever believe me."

"I don't believe you, either," Pedro said.

"So, anyway, to make a long story short – I'm tired today," Joey said putting his head back.

"That wasn't the long story?" Glenn quipped from the back, laughing.

Joey ignored him. "I need a neck pillow. You know those neck pillow things that look like a horseshoe? Those things are great," he continued to no one in particular. He was looking out the window. Is he talking to himself? "My head's flying all over the place. I need some support… a cocktail would be nice, too. A little cocktail and a neck pillow…"

Pedro, from the passenger seat, stretched over and looked at the odometer. "We've gone 97 miles so far. That's, what... less than 1% of the trip?" he said, smiling, with a hint of disbelief in his tone. He relaxed back in his seat shaking his head. "Shit, man. I'm already tired of driving."

Our first ballpark is brand new Citi Field in Flushing and we have to be there for a 1:30 game against the Brewers. Good match-up today – Santana vs. Gallardo – so we should be seeing a pitcher's duel.

But we're running late. Packing the Vanbino had taken longer than we had anticipated and since Pedro is the one with the lead foot, he got behind the wheel to make up some time.

Out of the four of us, Pedro is by far the most aggressive driver; a funny contrast to his character because he is also the quiet one, the most reserved one... the responsible one of the group. He doesn't say much but when he does, it's with conviction and passion and it means something. He's from the Dominican but was raised in West Philly and is one hell of a cameraman.

An exit sign for Trenton passes. It's 11:45 and we're still probably a good hour, hour fifteen south of the ballpark. We have some time to spare but you can never bet on New York traffic.

I look over and see the red rabbit's foot on our keychain dangling from the ignition. My dad had given it to us before we left.

"For good luck," he said. For a trip like this, we're going to need all the luck we can get.

24

From my front seat I see Glenn all the way in the back. He is staring out of the window, his eyes hiding behind his sunglasses. When it comes to baseball, Glenn is a walking encyclopedia. He is 42, the oldest of us four by 15 years. He often recalls with fondness the days his dad would take him to Connie Mack Stadium when he was a boy. Those trips to the old yard left a lasting impression on him and just a few years ago, he wrote and directed a documentary on Connie Mack Stadium. His experience in film and knowledge of baseball are invaluable to our little guerilla-film operation. Glenn has two kids, a fiancé, and elderly parents to look after back home (much more responsibility than any of us have) and I was surprised when he said he'd come along. I'm thankful to have him here.

As I sit in the company of the team of guys, I think about what it took just to get to *this* point – all the planning, the scheduling, the funding... that is an accomplishment in and of itself. The idea for 30in30 was hatched one night at my uncle's apartment with my cousin. What started out as an innocent little question grew into a life-consuming obsession with finding the answer if driving to all 30 Major League ballparks in 30 days to see a game in each one was possible. In the beginning, I never had any intentions of actually *doing* this Trip… I just liked talking about it. The more I talked about it, however, the more momentum it gained. It eventually gained so much steam that it moved faster than I could keep up with, sucked in other people, and before I knew it, I'm on the road actually *doing* it. 30in30 grew into something that was more powerful than any of us and now here we are.

It's 12:30 and we are in North Jersey. Manhattan is close.

The fifth member of our team is the 2009 Toyota Sienna mini-van we rented from Hertz. On the outside, she's sleek and shiny and silver like a bullet and inside, despite the occupancy of four grown men and all of their luggage, there is still some manageable leg room. With only 12,000 miles under her wheels, she was tuned and ready for her 18,000+ mile adventure across the country. In honor of the Great Bambino, we call her the Mini Vanbino.

I can now see the skyline of Manhattan rising majestically over the hills to our right and now we'll follow signs for the Lincoln Tunnel to take us through the heart of the city. The quickest way to get to Flushing, surprisingly, is to cut clear through Manhattan, ride along the southern edge of Central Park and then take the Queensboro Bridge over the East River and into Queens.

12:45pm

There was surprisingly little traffic for a Saturday afternoon in one of the busiest cities in the world and we ended up making it to Citi Field in plenty of time.

We took Northern Boulevard to 126th Street and I remember being able to see the Mets new ballpark long before we ever got there. It was huge and stood all alone in the middle of an enormous parking lot. Flushing Bay lay in the background and planes from LaGuardia fly low overhead.

We parked near a fenced-off mountain of rubble in the parking lot – steel beams protruding in all directions from blue, white, and orange-painted concrete – just to the side of Citi Field. A year ago, this was Shea. I had been to Shea a couple times and had never cared much for it, but there are a lot of people who called Shea home and walking passed I realized there is more then just concrete and steel in that heap – there are memories, as well.

We entered our Ballpark #1 through the Jackie Robinson Rotunda, an impressive entrance built in honor of one of the games most important players. The rotunda itself was modeled after the beloved Ebbets Field, Jackie's ballpark over in Brooklyn. I like what the Mets did with their new ballpark. When they were formed in 1962, the team took the colors blue and orange to pay tribute to the two beloved New York teams that no longer played in the boroughs – The New York Giants and the Brooklyn Dodgers. Now their ballpark pays tribute to those teams, from the Polo Grounds to Ebbets Field, from Willie Mays to Duke Snyder. It's beautiful and very classy but I wish there was a little more Mets history here since this is, after all, *their* home.

We found our seats up in Section 524, settled in and enjoyed our Shack Burgers. Right off the bat (no pun intended... seriously) we were treated to a great game, and, as expected, it was a pitching duel, but the Mets pulled it out and won 1-0. There will be many more low-scoring games like this here – the outfield is enormous!

4:15pm

Back on the road – the same road – but this time headed south. Our first ballpark is already in our rear-view mirror and now it's on to our second one – Citizens Bank Park in Philadelphia, our home park.

All four of us live in Philly and we are all Phillies fans so, even though we've been to the Bank countless times before, we're still excited. Friends and family are throwing us a send-off tailgate in the parking lot and by the time we arrived, the party was in full swing.

There was Tom, one of my best friends who I've known since kindergarten and the one person who truly made this Trip possible by contributing money to the Trip. Tom is going to meet up with us in California and go to some games with us out there.

There was my mom and dad and Wes, my brother, here to show their usual support for one of my endeavors (or, as my mom calls them – "shenanigans.")

"Here's the confirmation in case you need it when you get there," my mom said handing me a printed receipt. She had already booked us a room in the Marriott Waterfront Hotel in San Diego, our last stop, as a "Congratulations-you-did-it!" gift.

"What if we don't make it, though, Mom?"

"I have a good feeling you will," and she squeezed my arm.

"Where's Glenn?" I asked Pedro. I just realized I haven't seen him in a while.

Pedro points with a nod of his head. Across the parking lot in a corner garden area, I see Glenn talking on his phone and pacing back and forth behind a giant shrub.

"What's he doing?" Wes asked.

"He's on Fire Island," Joey informs us in a matter-of-fact tone then takes a bite of hotdog as he continues to watch Glenn.

Fire Island? Never heard of it. I turn to Wes and ask him with my eyes if he knows. He returns the look and shrugs.

"What's Fire Island?" I ask Joey.

Joey turns to me. "Fire Island?" he asks, seemingly surprised that we don't know what it is. "It's that place where you go when you're on the phone with your significant other. Everything else around you in the real world doesn't matter anymore and you become vacant from that world, just a ghost of your former self wandering aimlessly…"

"Very poetic, man," I tell him.

"Thanks." He looks at Glenn and shakes his head like a sympathetic doctor diagnosing a disease. "He's got Fire Island. He's got it bad. It's hot there… gets real steamy," he continues and takes another bite of his hotdog. "Look at him – he's walking around like an idiot in the bushes, no idea where he is right now. Completely out of touch with his surroundings and you know why? Cause he's not here – he's on Fire Island." He takes a sip of his beer. "Pedro will be visiting Fire Island, just you wait. You and I, though, we don't have to worry about that, thank God. We're safe." He takes another sip of beer as the three of us watch Glenn on Fire Island.

Tailgating with everyone was such a good time that we didn't end up making it into Citizens Bank Park until the 4th inning. I was stuffed from all the burgers and brats and beer from the tailgate but that didn't stop me from getting a Schmitter when I got inside. I had to – this trip, after all, is about experiencing the ballparks and all the sights, sounds, and tastes that go along with them. One of the neat things about each ballpark is that each one – from their architecture to their cuisine – reflects a bit of the local flavor of the city they reside in. Each one has a signature food they are known for and we're planning on trying it all. I now sit face-to-face with the Schmitter sandwich, dripping its greasy goodness all over my pants.

"How much do you weigh?" I ask Joey, Pedro, and Glenn, not looking up from my sandwich.

"156," Pedro said. "I just weighed myself yesterday."

"I dunno, like 160? 165?" Joey guesses.

Glenn looks at us disgusted then chuckles. "I'm 190!"

"You're old, though," Joey says.

I look down at the Schmitter and the Schmitter stares back up at me. It's a glorious sandwich – grilled steak, pork roll, cheese, onions, and tomatoes packed into a Kaiser roll. For the next month, our diets, cholesterol, and overall health, I'd say, were no doubt going to take a serious hit. "Well… no turning back now," I thought and bit into the sandwich. Though it's probably a couple days worth of calories on one bun and definitely a heart attack or two, I highly recommend it. You only live once, right?

Our seats once again were way up high, up in 415. We'll be getting the cheapest seats available at these games to conserve some money. It didn't bother us any – we love watching the games, but this road trip after all was all about experiencing the ball*park* more than it was about the ball*game*.

Up in our seats, we watched in horror as Lidge gave up four runs in the ninth to the Padres and was dealt his first blown save in his last 49 attempts. This is the first time he's blown a save since September of '07!

As we were leaving the ballpark that night, they played a recording of Harry singing his famous, traditional rendition of "High Hopes"… I still can't believe he's gone. It's only been five days and it still doesn't feel real. That deep, distinct voice, charred to a regal baritone by years of cigarettes, had been *the* voice of Phillies baseball – the only one I have known for as long as I've been alive – and now that voice is silent.

> *High hopes*
> *He's got high hopes*
> *He's got high apple pie*
> *In the sky hopes*

I know it's crazy but I couldn't help but feel like Harry was singing that song for us.

10:30pm

Our first two ballparks are in the bag but our first day is long from over. Tomorrow we have Yankee Stadium at 1:05 and we want to get there early to explore so we decided it best to drive back up to New York and stay with a couple of friends of mine tonight.

So once again, for the third time today, we merged back onto the Jersey Turnpike. At this point, I've been awake for 16 hours, driven over 250 miles, seen two ballgames and we still have about an hour and 45 minutes of driving ahead of us before we can sleep. This will be our routine, though, so I'm going to have to get used to it. There'll be a lot more days and nights like this one in the coming month.

With the Philly skyline still in sight, we were heading north when Glenn dropped the bomb on us.

"Guys, I can't do this... I just can't," he said in a somber voice from the middle pilot seat. "I thought I could but I can't leave."

Was he joking? We're not even finished our first day!

"A month away from home is just too long," he continued. Like I said before, Glenn is the oldest one out of the four of us, and with two kids, a fiancé and elderly parents to look after, he has far more responsibility than the three of us have. Leaving all of that was asking too much of him, and I understood.

We detoured from the route that had become so familiar on this first day and we crossed the Delaware River into Jersey. Glenn lives with his fiancé in the Philadelphia suburbs and when we pulled up in front of his house, it was pitch dark.

We all got out and as Pedro, Joey, and myself said good-bye to Glenn in the blinking, red brake lights of the Vanbino, I patted him on the back to let him know it's okay.

"I'm sorry guys. Sorry I'm lettin' ya down," he said.

"Don't be sorry... this is good what you're doing. You gotta do what you gotta do," Joey reassured him.

And, with his bag in one arm and his pillow under the other, he started up the front walk to his house and we watched him disappear into the night.

Was I angry? No... shocked, more than anything... but certainly not angry. Worried, I think though, above all else. At that point in the Trip, I didn't know if it would be possible to accomplish all the demands of driving and filming a movie with just the three of us. Time would tell, though, and for now all we can do is carry on. Our motto for the Trip, after all, is "whatever it takes."

"Fire Island," Joey said as we pulled away. "Got him."

2:00am

It had been a long day of getting our feet wet, of trying to familiarize ourselves with our new routine and with each other. In a time where we were about to spend every hour for the next 30 days together, and whether we liked it or not, we had to learn each others habits, how each one thought, reacted, saw, moved. I had wanted four guys on the Trip because I didn't think three guys alone could conquer all the driving and filming that this project demanded.

But now we have no choice. We had very little margin for error before losing Glenn and now being a man down, we have even less.

Tonight, we're staying with a couple of my good friends from high school – Jackie and Jill, sisters who now live together in Queens. The Glenn detour set us back and we didn't reach their apartment until after two in the morning. I was physically and emotionally drained and I don't remember ever having been more tired in my life than I was at that moment when I stepped into the apartment.

The last thing I remember from that night was dropping my bag by the couch and sitting down.

Sunday, April 19 — DAY 2
The Bronx, New York
1:05 Game @ Yankee Stadium (Ballpark #3)
Total Miles Today — 104
Total Miles So Far — 434

8:00am

     Pedro woke me on the couch that morning. Luckily he had set an alarm because I had not. It was weird – as tired as I was last night and managing only five hours of sleep, I was surprisingly awake and ready to go.

     Jackie and Jill brought some egg sandwiches and coffee home from a little deli on Steinway for the three of us...

     ...the three of us...

Not even a full day into the Trip and we're already a man down. Was this Trip doomed to fail from the start? It hasn't been an ideal beginning but there's no turning back now. And, hey – we're still on schedule.

Before leaving for the Bronx that morning, we needed to take care of the Vanbino. The departure of Glenn had freed up a considerable amount of space and it was already really messy. We really just needed to organize our food and equipment a little better.

11:00am

We wanted to leave ourselves plenty of time to explore the much-hyped, brand new Yankee Stadium. Like its NL counterpart in Flushing, this, too, was the Opening Season for the new ballpark.

I have mixed feelings about the new Yankee Stadium. I'm a sucker for history and hated to see the original Yankee Stadium, a classic ballpark that was the home to so many greats, be replaced by a shiny, new one. Though the field dimensions are the same and the exterior was modeled after the original 1923 park, I'm afraid the feeling in the air will be different. When you sat in the seats of the old park, you could feel the history in the air. Ruth, Gehrig, DiMaggio, Mantle played ON THAT FIELD. There was a certain intangible presence inside that old ballpark that cannot be replicated. For all the money that was spent on the new stadium, for all the luxuries and all the modern amenities the old park lacked, there was one thing that could not be bought that made the old Yankee Stadium the real Yankee Stadium – the magic.

We walked past the old Yankee Stadium on our way to the new one. It's still standing but it might as well not be. It looks withered and defeated like a grizzled, old veteran whose spotlight has faded and now stands in the shadow of a bright and promising new rookie. The crumbling walls are being picked away by souvenir-hungry fans wanting a tiny piece of history on their shelf.

We entered the new park through the Great Hall, which had to be no less than three stories high, column-lined and all marble and then walked out to the ground level around the field to explore. I passed by a restaurant behind home plate with white linen-covered tables. Really? At a ballpark? What would Ruth think?

2:35pm

We're way up high about 12, 15 rows from the top, first base side. Wes is here – he is a college student who lives in Manhattan and when I told him I suddenly had an extra ticket for the game (Glenn's) he hopped on the train and met us at the ballpark.

"I'm not impressed," I told him. "For all the hype and money, I'm not impressed." I know what you're thinking – who makes me the judge? As a fan of baseball, I feel that I'm qualified to judge, just like you are, too. The ballpark, after all, is *for* the fan, and *as* a fan, I am just not comfortable here. It's too big, it's too corporate; Joey said it best when he compared it to a government building or a bank. And with all the columns, marble, and gold trim, he's right. My fears had been confirmed – there is no magic here. All the great players of the Yankees past had left their grace behind and you could feel their aura in the air when you watched a ballgame at the old Yankee Stadium. It had spirit and it had soul. But not here and not anymore. When it comes to baseball, 9 times out of 10 I'll vote in favor of tradition and although the most storied franchise in all of sports call this home, it lacks just that – tradition. It lacks the character and the charm that its predecessor across the street had, and still has, within its deteriorating walls. It lacks that certain intangible.

"You're just an old-fashioned douche," my brother said. "This place is nice."

Well, tomorrow is Fenway so if it's tradition I want then it's tradition I'm going to get… and a damn healthy dose of it.

4:50pm

We were walking along the outside of Old Yankee Stadium on our way to the parking garage when a wiffle ball fell from the sky and landed in front of us.

"Little help?" yelled a guy from the top deck of the garage. Joey picked up the plastic ball, wound up, and threw it with all his might. The garage has three decks… and three decks are apparently *just* out of Joey's range because the ball just missed clearing the fence that surrounds the top deck.

Joey picked the ball up again and wound up… and again it was just short.

"Come on! Little more muscle!" yelled the kid from the deck who was now accompanied by his buddy, both of whom wear Yankees hats.

"Give it to me. Let me try," I say, confident that I can make it up there. It doesn't look that high.

I take the ball, plant my feet and cock back my arm. I rifle the ball with every ounce of strength that I can muster and watch it zoom past the first deck, fly past the second and soar up to the third. Then it dies as it lightly taps the fence and falls back to earth.

"Damn, that's harder than it looks," I say.

"Yeah, no shit," Joey replies, rubbing his shoulder.

"We'll be right up!" I yell to the guys.

Up on the third deck of the garage, we meet Tim, John and Eric. We hand them their ball back.

"What do you think of the new Yankee Stadium?" I ask John who holds the thin, yellow wiffle ball bat in his hand. He wears a Sabathia jersey and a hat with the Red Sox "B" on it but besides the "B" are the letters "L-O-W-S."

"Love it! Love. It."

Eric takes the bat and shouts his answer as he strolls towards the fence. "The old one was nice but this one is great!" He takes his batters stance just in front of the fence.

"This guy sucks. Watch this strike," John says. Tim trots out to patrol the outfield for any fly balls. John pitches one in and Eric makes contact but pops a foul up, behind him, and back over the fence.

"Alright, we're out of here. You guys are on your own for this one," Joey says.

Tim, John, and Eric are all 28 years old, have all known each other since kindergarten, and always come to Yankees games together. After every game, they play some wiffle ball on the top deck of the parking garage in the shadows of the old Yankee Stadium. And as we walk away, I now see the venerable yard in a different light than I did when we arrived. There it stands majestically behind the wiffle ball game serving as a backdrop for a lifelong tradition for these fans. It seems proud, content for the memories it has served fans like Tim, John, and Eric and the role it has played in history.

5:15pm

I wanted to make a couple stops before hitting the road up to Boston. First, we stopped at the site where the Polo Grounds once stood, right across the Hudson River from Yankee Stadium. An apartment complex stands here now but a cement staircase from the old ballpark still remains intact scaling the hill to the Polo Grounds apartment complex. I wonder how many people walk down these steps every day having no idea what they were originally built for? And, most importantly, right here, right here on this land where I stand, the very first hotdog was sold. They were called red-hots back then.

"Het-deg, hee-yeh!" Joey yelled in his best ballpark hotdog vendor impersonation. A couple at the top of the steps quickly looked down at him. He sounds like a squealing cat when he does that voice and I can't imagine what those people are thinking. I can't help but chuckle.

Then after the Polo Grounds, we stopped briefly in Hoboken. There is a plaque at the intersection of 11th and Washington smack dab in the middle of a neighborhood that marks the spot of the Elysian Fields where the very first baseball game ever was played. (There has since been evidence of baseball being played earlier in Pittsfield, Massachusetts as early as 1791), but the game played here on the Elysian Fields is regarded as the first game played with the modern rules outlined by Alexander Cartwright.

Interesting – 'elysian' is a synonym for 'paradise'…. I wonder who named the Elysian Fields? Giamatti must have surely loved that name… very appropriate.

Now, you may be asking, "Travis, why do you care about seeing some crumbling old steps and a little plaque?"

Because I'm a nerd. So what? Deal with it.

10:18pm

We were stopped at a gas station on the doorsteps of Boston when we met Ball in the House, a traveling beat-box band out of Massachusetts. They approached us first when they saw the 30 BALLPARKS IN 30 DAYS magnet on the side of the Vanbino.

"How many you guys seen?"

"We just started yesterday," Pedro told them. "We saw Citi Field, Citizens Bank and Yankee and now we're on our way to Fenway tomorrow."

"That is awesome, man!" All three of them wore Red Sox hats.

"You guys Sox fans, huh?" I asked them.

"Oh, hardcore, man! Live and breathe Sox baseball," he said in a thick Boston accent.

We talked for a while and when we found out they were a beat-box band, we wondered if they could do a rendition of "Take Me Out To the Ballgame" beat-box style. They had never done it before but these guys were pros and they didn't mess around. Pedro set the camera and the bass vocalist and the drum guy went at it, improvising the whole way and it was amazing. I must have played the recording back from the tape a hundred times – I couldn't get enough. It was definitely one of the coolest things I have ever heard.

Like the game of wiffle ball outside Yankee Stadium, this little surprise encounter was neat. After the months of planning leading up to the Trip, it was refreshing to have something random like this happen.

"You guys picked a good day to go to Fenway, too," the lead singer told us.

"Why's that?" Pedro asked.

"It's Patriot's Day and Marathon Monday. It's a holiday up there and everybody parties in the street!"

"Oh, is that why the game is at 11?" I ask, finally making sense of it. I remember thinking when planning the schedule that an 11:05am start time was an unusual time for a game.

"Yeah," he said. "Used to be the Marathon would end at Fenway and then the Sox would play. They've since adjusted the marathon and it doesn't work out that way anymore but the Sox still play at 11 and it's still a great day to be in the city. Whatever you do, though, don't drive. Park outside the city and take the T in. You'll never make it if you try and drive."

11:03pm

We arrived at my friend's apartment in Boston after a long first two days. We were beat and tomorrow would be a long day, as well, so we got to sleep as soon as we could.

But poor Pedro – he's allergic to cats and my friend here has two.

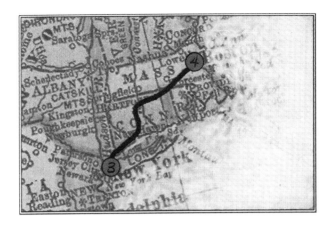

Monday, April 20 — DAY 3
Boston
11:05 Game @ Fenway Park (Ballpark #4)
Total Miles Today — 211
Total Miles So Far — 645

6:30am

I already showered but fell back asleep *sitting up* in the kitchen chair while waiting for Pedro. I'm pretty sure that's the first time I've ever done that...

Today is going to be a good day – we have our first radio interview at Mix 98.1 on the Karson & Kennedy Show and we actually get to go into the studio for this! Then after the interview, we have Fenway – the ballpark at the top of my bucket list.

The interview went great. I was nervous at first but Joey saved me. He's a natural – well-spoken and concise, quick and witty with some of his classic catchphrases sprinkled in. When asked to sum up the trip, he told the audience, "it's like an all-you-can-eat buffet and we're eating everything." Karson and Kennedy loved that line.

"So wait, did you guys buy four tickets for today's game??" Kennedy asked anxiously after learning that Glenn had dropped out.

"Yeah, we have an extra one," I said

"What are doing with it?" Kennedy said in a tone that hinted she was interested.

I smiled. "Nothing now... you want it?"

"Hell yeah I want it!" she yelled with excitement.

"It's yours," I tell her.

"But you're gonna have to sit with us, you know," Joey said.

"If it's just for a few hours, I'll be able to deal," Kennedy said laughing.

10:12am

Thank God we listened to the advice from Ball In the House and took the train in because the streets are a mess... I don't even know if there are any that are actually open. I mean, just people everywhere. Mobs and mobs of them. It took us a good thirty minutes to walk the block and a half from the T stop to Fenway. Just throngs of people everywhere.

"Where the hell is it?" Joey asked about Fenway.

"I don't know. It's around here somewhere," I said trying to navigate through the crowds.

As I stepped up to the corner I glanced left and I saw the green light towers of Fenway poking up into the sky above the roofs of the neighboring bars and restaurants. We had entered Red Sox Nation and the atmosphere was electric.

We passed by the Cask and Flagon and made our way down Lansdowne Street along the outside of Fenway. I touched the cinder wall below a sign that said 'Bleacher B' – this place, this ballpark, Fenway, is not only the heart of this party but is a mecca for baseball fans and now here I am, standing in its shadow. Regardless if you love or hate the Red Sox, if you're a fan of baseball then this is a place you have to visit.

Before going in, however, Kennedy had told us this morning that we had to visit the Sausage Guy – not the Sausage *Man*, not the Sausage *King* – but the Sausage *Guy*. Very specific instructions. Apparently, his sausages are the best and, although many try, there are no substitutes. After finding his little grill stand on Lansdowne, I got an Italian sausage with grilled peppers and onions and let me tell you – Kennedy was right – it *was* amazing.

Then we made our way onto Ipswitch Street, passed the famous Ted Williams statue, and approached the turnstiles of Gate B.

Here we go.

Memories from Rickwood flashed through my head as I stepped through the gate. Just like at Rickwood, stepping into Fenway was literally stepping into a time capsule and you were instantly transported to another era. Everything just changed. It's a different world in here with a different feeling in the air. It was like hearing The Beatles or Led Zeppelin for the first time – something deep inside of me stirred... feelings that had gone unfelt until now awoke.

Out in the right field grandstand, Kennedy met us at our seats which are just slabs of wood with wrought iron armrests. The seats are small and rickety and rather uncomfortable. And also, with a view obstructed by a support beam, I feel like I should be saying Fenway sucked.

But it didn't suck at all. In fact, it was great. In the "inconveniences" is where the charm of it all lives and it is this that adds to the ambience. It is that certain intangible that makes Fenway *Fenway*. I don't know how else to describe the feeling in the air.

Sitting in that horrible seat, I couldn't help but think of all the generations of people who have sat here before me, all the passionate fans who have suffered through the curse of the Bambino, and all the fans whose loyalty was finally rewarded in '04 for the first time in 86 years.

Fenway Park opened on April 12, 1912, and was scheduled to be front page news but was pushed to the back when the Titanic sank just a few days before. I thought about that. How long ago the Titanic sank and how much has happened, how much has changed in the world in the close to 100 years that has passed. Through Prohibition, a Great Depression, World Wars and assassinations, Model T's to Lamborghinis, Morse code to Facebook, everything in the world has progressed, deteriorated, grown, developed, collapsed and rebuilt... everything on the outside has changed.

But not in here.

In here, nothing has changed at all. It's as if time stands still. I'm sitting in the same wooden seat that a fan 80 years ago could have sat in and I'm coming to the park for the same reason, too. Once you're in here, nothing on the outside world matters. And if, by some miraculous disruption in the relativities of time and space that allowed me to sit next to a Sox fan from 80 years ago at a ballgame, we would not be strangers. Despite our generations separated by almost a century, we would have common ground to walk on because we'd be talking about baseball, and baseball hasn't changed.

James Earl Jones said it best – "The one constant through all the years, Ray, has been baseball. America has rolled by like an army of steamrollers. It has been erased like a blackboard, rebuilt and erased again. But baseball has marked the time."

Gives me chills just thinking about that. For all the anticipation about Fenway that had been building in me for years, this venerable ballpark did not disappoint.

I am happy.

We're on our way to McGreevy's, known as America's first sports bar. They advertise as being only 1,200 steps from Fenway, but it took us a good 45 minutes to get there. Boylston Street was still packed with people from Marathon crowds so McGreevy's felt a lot longer away than 1,200 steps, but I don't know... I didn't count. Maybe I was distracted by the group of guys running in their thong underwear high-fiving the cheering crowd?

McGreevy's is owned by the Dropkick Murphy's and it was jamming. We happened to start talking to the distribution manager of Narragansett Beer, a local beer up here in Boston. We told him about our 30in30 trip and after that, we didn't pay for a single beer all night. He also introduced us to Scruffy Wallace, the lead bagpipe for the Dropkick Murphy's. Scruffy talked passionately about the Red Sox and told us why Fenway is the best ballpark in America. He was poetic and eloquent in his words and it was apparent that this was a subject he frequently discussed.

"For me, best thing about Fenway is that baseball and history live and breathe there. You can go to a museum or a library and read about heroes and look at pictures of them but when you go down to Fenway Park, you're actually in history, you know?" A pause and a slight smile from him. "It's everything baseball was meant to be at Fenway Park. Even the smell and the environment when you go in is unmistakable... there is no other park, anywhere, like Fenway Park."

The way he looked at me told me that he's never known anything to be more true than that. His conviction, his passion, his sincere and genuine love for his ballpark

50

summed up perfectly the attitude of the fans in Red Sox Nation.

12:30am

Thanks to Mr. Narragansett Guy, we were a little drunk when we left McGreevy's but we somehow found our way back to my friend's place and crashed immediately.

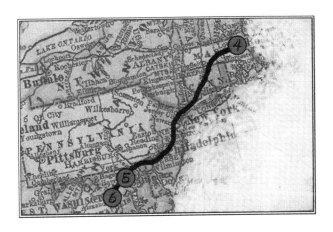

7:30am

    "What'd you guys think of the Fenway Franks?" I asked from the passenger's seat.

    "Eh, nothing special," Joey said from the back. "The roll was good but nothing special." Pedro nodded in agreement. We also got some clam chowder from Legal Sea Foods. I don't like clams or clam chowder but Pedro and Joey said it was delicious.

    Today was going to be interesting.

When we made our schedule, Baltimore was originally a 1:00 game and DC was scheduled for a 7:30 game. Perfect! But in the weeks between then and now, the Baltimore game was rescheduled for a 7:30 start time. It screwed us. There was no other day we could get to Camden Yards in the Trip, so we had to make do with the situation and split the games up. Since Baltimore is north of DC, we decided to hit that up first, leave in the third or fourth inning, drive the 40 minutes to DC, then catch the second half of the Nationals game. It isn't ideal but we have no other choice. And on top of that, we've been following a storm system that may complicate matters…

It poured last night. There has been storms all up and down the eastern seaboard this whole week and it's not supposed to clear up anytime soon.

Joey got on his phone and checked the forecast for Baltimore and DC today – late afternoon and evening thunderstorms. Rain heavy at times. Chance of precip 100%.

Fantastic.

It's a 7.5 hour drive to Baltimore so we were on the road by 8:30. I took the first leg of the trip because Pedro's allergies were kicking his ass and Joey… well, Joey had more Narragansett last night than we did.

I visit Camden Yards a lot since it is so close to Philly but I still look forward to it every time I come. It opened in '92 and its success reversed the unfortunate trend of those concrete, multi-purpose stadiums that opened during the 60's, 70's, and 80's. Its retro-modern design has influenced every park that has opened in its wake and all the fan-friendly amenities and great ballpark food that we enjoy today we owe to Oriole Park in Baltimore. So next time you're at your ballpark, give a toast to Camden Yards.

12:30pm

I pulled into a rest stop and when I took the keys from the ignition I noticed the rabbit's foot was missing. I searched the van but came up empty.

"Shit," I said under my breath. I didn't mention it to the guys.

3:45pm

We arrived in Baltimore a little ahead of schedule (Pedro and his lead foot drove the second shift so that probably had something to do with it). The skies are sunny and clear right now but the forecast hasn't changed.

We parked the Vanbino, coincidentally, on the same block as the Bambino's childhood home so we stopped in. I forget what we paid for admission but it wasn't much. The place is full of memorabilia, archives, and trivia that shape the story of Ruth's childhood and it's well worth it for any baseball fan to check out. Also, it's only two blocks from Camden Yards. Here's a little fun fact for ya – the Babe's father owned a bar way back in the day when the Babe was a little boy. The bar's former location? Left field in Camden Yards.

Across the road from Camden Yards on the other side of Eislen Street, there's a small row of bars that close off the street to traffic and throw a block party before every Orioles home game. There are tents set up with food and beer and there's people everywhere. It's a great scene and what's nice is that you're allowed to bring the food you buy out here into the ballpark with you.

Wild Bill runs a grill at this block party and he serves up sausages and brats, meatballs and burgers and they all look amazing. But we got what Wild Bill is best known for – the crab cake sandwich.

It's a delicacy, a work of art.

Joey spiced his up a bit with some Old Bay and ketchup and bit into it. "Unbelievable. Anywhere you go this would cost you 37 bucks... look at all that crab!"

He was right. It was pure crab – no filler. And it wasn't one of those little hockey puck-sized crab cakes, either. This one is massive – about the size of a DVD but with the thickness of a filet mignon. If you like crab cakes – even if you *don't* like crab cakes – do yourself a favor and go meet Wild Bill. He'll treat you right.

"It's getting' ready to raaaaiiiin..." Wild Bill said rather melodically after we went back to tell him how his crab cakes changed our life. I looked up to the sky. Dark storm clouds are rolling in from the west.

We walked down Eutew Street to the sound of thunder rolling in the distance. The storm was coming in fast.

"Aw, nice! Free tee-shirt day!" Pedro said excitedly on the other side of the turnstile.

"Nice. First giveaway," I said holding mine up to look at it. I adopted the Orioles as my AL team a few years back because I wanted a team in the AL to root for, too. I chose the Orioles for a lot of reasons – they're close enough to Philly to drive to and see some home games, they have an awesome ballpark, they have a great history, a passionate fan base, and, currently, they suck. I don't want to be jumping on the bandwagon. (I almost went with the A's because of their Philly roots but they're all the way out in California and I'd never be able to go to any games.) So the O's it was.

"Shit... tarp's on the field," Joey said as the field came into view. "Shit! This is the worst thing that can happen."

"Maybe it won't rain. The tarp is down as just a precaution. I think they'll at least start the game," I reasoned.

I should've kept my fat mouth shut because as I was getting the last word out, I felt a drop hit my forehead.

Then another... and another...

Then all of a sudden it was a downpour.

People scattered like ants under a lifted rock and we ran to a roof along the B&O Warehouse for shelter. Joey took out his phone to check the Doppler.

"Shit. This is not good," he said. "It's a big storm that's coming through. And it sucks because they didn't even start the game which might mean the chances of a PPD are better."

"What do we do if the Nats game is on? How long do we wait here?" I ask them.

"Checking the Nats now..." Joey scrolls through his phone. "Nats game in a delay, too."

"Okay," I say. "We'll have to keep a close eye on that game and see if they start before this one. Because if they start in DC and this one is still in a delay, we're gonna have to leave and go there so at least we only miss one game and not *two*, ya know? And then if it comes to that, we're gonna have to figure out when to come back here... maybe next week on our way south?"

"Let's hope they're not *both* postponed," Pedro said.

"Then I think we'll be totally screwed. There's no way we'll be able to make up *two* games," I said.

8:45pm

We're still in a delay and it's still pouring. If there's any silver lining here, it's that the Nats game is still in a delay, too, and that neither one has been postponed yet.

There's still hope.

58

Forty minutes south of us in DC, the Nats game just got under way. I don't know how much longer we wait here. At some point, we have to cut our losses.

We're up in our section, very last row at the top under the awning to stay dry. It's still raining… scratch that – *pouring* – as I look out onto the tarp-covered field. Flashbacks of Rickwood run through my mind. The Trip has barely gotten started and now it's already in danger of ending. Could we really fail this quickly? I knew weather would be our biggest enemy but it's only the *fifth day!* The line between ambition and stupidity is becoming clearer.

I chew on sunflower seeds and glance over at Pedro, his new O's shirt wrapped around his head like a towel. I glance at Joey and he scrolls through his phone.

"I think we're gonna be okay here. The forecast says clearing by 9:00 and it's…" he looks up at the big clock in centerfield, "… well, it's past 9:00 right now. But it should be stopping any minute."

Finally, for the first time in two hours, the rain has stopped. Scattered applause from the little pockets of remaining fans sounded as the grounds crew ran onto the field to clean up. Over two hours behind schedule, we were finally going to see some baseball.

As Brad Bergesen delivered his first pitch to Chris Getz, the Nats game 45 minutes away entered the second inning. We couldn't stay here long. We were already flirting with disaster and the Beltway between the two cities is notorious for traffic.

We don't want to push our luck tonight, especially since our rabbit's foot has gone missing.

9:50pm

We got to the Vanbino and put Pedro behind the wheel – we needed to fly! And as we sat there with light raindrops sprinkling on the windshield, we could not figure out how to program the address for Nationals Park into our Garmin.

We're wasting time that we don't have.

"Dude, how the hell do you program DC into this thing?" I ask to whoever wants to answer. "It needs a state but DC isn't a state."

"Type in Maryland," Pedro says.

No luck. Virginia, maybe? I frantically type that but no good.

"It's not picking up DC," I report.

"I'm going on Google," Joey says as he takes out his laptop. He has one of those broadband connectors so we can access the internet but it's proven to be really spotty so far.

"Just start heading south… I dunno, just head south," I told Pedro. He starts driving.

"What am I looking for?" he asks.

"I dunno. I guess just any highway sign that says south."

"What's the address?" Joey asks.

"1500 South Capitol Street Southeast, Washington, DC, DC," I read. What the hell? South, Southeast, DC, DC? I don't think that makes sense... does it?

By sheer luck, Pedro ran into a sign for 295-S. That sounded familiar. We jumped on that.

"Service is spotty... stand by," Joey reports. I feel helpless and lost when the Garmin is ill-communicato. I think I even have minor anxiety attacks when it's not on. (Sorry, is that too dramatic?)

Pedro continued down 295 looking for signs to DC. He was easily touching 100. How many tickets do you think Pedro will get before this is all said and done?

"Hey, guys," Pedro asks with some urgency in his voice. "Guys which way?" Just up ahead, the highway splits – 295 goes off to the left, 201 to the right. No signs for DC.

Joey frantically tries to refresh his internet connection.

"What do I do guys??" Pedro asks even more urgently. He stays in the left hand lane following 295. The split is about 50 yards ahead.

"Google up!" Joey announces triumphantly from the back. The split is here and a thin but quickly thickening strip of median begins to separate us from 201.

"RIGHT! RIGHT!" Joey shouts.

Pedro yanks the wheel to the right and by some miracle that I still don't understand, we did not flip. The Vanbino flew across the two right lanes of 295 towards the quickly disappearing 201 – the window of opportunity to merge almost shut. We were driving down the median, bouncing so high in our seats that our heads were hitting the padded ceiling, torn grass and mud flying violently in our wake. I grasped the handle on my armrest like I was on some wild roller coaster careening out of control... because this was not any different.

But Pedro... Pedro somehow remained calm and cool and confident like he was in complete control the entire time.

We made the merge.

And as the Vanbino coasted down the middle lane of 201 like a boat on a calm sea after a storm, I looked over to Pedro, our captain. He stared straight ahead through the windshield like he's done that a thousand times before. Had he done that a thousand times before? I wouldn't doubt it. Still wide-eyed in horror, I peered back at Joey who sat there just as wide-eyed as me. We were both in disbelief, both in a minor state of shock of what just happened and how close we had seemingly come to death.

"I told you to buckle your seat belts," Pedro said calmly, keeping his cool gaze through the windshield. And then he spit out a sunflower shell.

Luckily there was no traffic because if there was, we would have not just been late but we would have probably died on Pedro's Wild Ride.

We entered through the left field gate by the statues of Walter Johnson and Frank Howard, passed the blooming cherry blossom trees and sat in the first section we saw. It wasn't our section but the usher could care less – it was empty tonight and he let us pick our seats.

"Wheww," I let out a sigh of relief after sitting down in a rain-soaked seat. We made it. The Trip would live on to see another day. We sat in silence for a while, catching our breath, thanking our luck, not really even noticing the light rain that was falling. Someone was on our side... somehow we made it. The game was in the 7th inning but it didn't matter – we made it. Ballpark #6 was in the bag.

"What is DC? I still don't get it... like technically what is it if it's not a state?" I ask.

"It's a district," Joey says. "It's a district of Columbia."

I don't think he knows what he's talking about. "I don't know what that means," I tell him.

He turns to me. "Columbia has a district and Washington is that district. It's a district, not a state."

Okay, now I'm positive he doesn't know what he's talking about.

"Wanna get some chili?" Pedro asks.

"Yeah," I say.

Ben's Chili Bowl is a DC landmark and when the Nationals opened their new park, they brought one in. The chili, fresh and steaming, warmed my bones on this chilly, wet, raw night.

After the game, we had to clean up the Vanbino. Pedro's Wild Ride had turned everything upside-down and inside-out and everything was thrown all over.

"Jesus! It looks like Wal-Mart threw-up in here," Joey said as he opened the side door. Pedro just laughed.

"Alright... Amp time," Joey said. He uncovered his stash of energy drinks from the havoc and cracked one open. Tomorrow was another doubleheader day – 1:05 in Pittsburgh then a 7:05 in Cleveland – so we figured it would be best to drive through the night so we can be in Pittsburgh by morning.

Joey sat in the drivers seat programming the Garmin. "I think I'm gonna call her the Babe," Joey announced with a little smirk.

I looked at him. "What are you talking about?"

"The Garmin. I'm gonna call her the Babe, ya know? She's got a sexy voice... it soothes me. I like her."

3:30am

I awoke as we pulled into a rest stop. The couple street lamps by the bathroom huts were the only source of light; beyond that, complete darkness. I had no idea where we were.

"We're only about 45 minutes from Pittsburgh," Joey said. "I figured we're close enough… I wanna get a little shut-eye."

"Sounds good," I said. It's awkward sleeping in a car seat and comfort is hard to find but I repositioned the balled-up sweatshirt under my head and did the best I could. The one thing that I forgot to pack was my pillow. I can't believe I forgot my pillow.

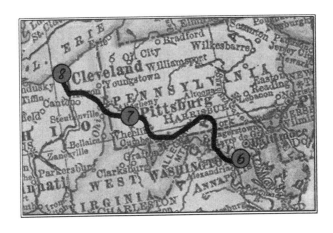

Wednesday, April 22 — DAY 5
Doubleheader Day #3 — Pittsburgh & Cleveland
1:05 Game @ PNC Park (Ballpark #7)
7:05 Game @ Progressive Field (Ballpark #8)
Total Miles Today — 380
Total Miles So Far — 1,473

10:30am

We're meeting Brian O'Neill at PNC today. He's a reporter for the Pittsburgh Post-Gazette who heard about our Trip somewhere online and is interested in writing a column on it. I spoke with him on the phone yesterday and he let us in on a little-known Pittsburgh secret...

"Turn here?" Pedro asked.

I stretch my head forward to see the street sign. "Yeah, I guess. This is where Brian said." We were on a dirt road surrounded by factories. "This is weird," but we proceeded anyway. Then out of nowhere, the Allegheny appeared and at the end of our road was a parking lot, a dock, and a boat.

"Sweet! There it is."

"I knew Brian wouldn't steer us wrong," Joey said from the back.

It was a cold morning in Pittsburgh and we were the only ones on the water taxi. The Pirates have trouble drawing fans even on warm summer nights so I doubt the park, on a cold, windy, Tuesday afternoon in April with a threat of serious storms, will be crowded.

"I'll take a Lager," Joey said to a crew lady as he was getting out some cash. He turned to Pedro and me. "You guys want one?"

"Yeah, I'll take one," I told him.

Joey cracked his open and took a long, slow sip and swallowed. "Mmm... that's good." We haven't had anything to eat yet today so I guess this was our breakfast.

"We don't see many Pirates fans on here," the Captain told us. "I mean, we get some, sure, especially in the middle of the season, but we make most of our money off Steelers fans. It's nice because fans can park down here then ride right to the stadiums and they don't have to worry about traffic afterwards."

"You guys pretty full for Steelers games, huh?" Joey asked.

"You bet," the Captain said.

I was sitting on a bench in the back of the small boat looking out at the passing scenery. What a view you get from here! The downtown skyline is just to our left, Heinz Field and the Heinz factory just to our right, and all these yellow bridges that span the river are so cool looking. Then PNC came into view sitting on the bank of the river just behind Heinz.

This water taxi is great. It's only about a 20-minute ride and it's only three bucks for a roundtrip. You don't have to pay for parking, you don't have to worry about traffic, so, yeah – I'd say the boat ride is worth it. PNC has its own dock on the Allegheny and the water taxi drops you off right there, so when you dock, you walk up some steps and you're literally right there *at* the ballpark.

"What about 30in30, but instead of *driving* the whole way, we take a *boat* the whole way…" Joey suggested.

"Dude, we don't even know if the driving one is possible!" Pedro said laughing.

"I dunno, man. That I think might be impossible. Cause like Coors in Denver… I don't think there's a river near there, ya know?" I said.

The sky was growing more ominous by the minute and it was looking more and more like the skies in Baltimore from yesterday. The wind was picking up, too, and as more black clouds rolled in, the sun disappeared and I was cold even in my heavy winter jacket, scarf, and snowcap. Thunderstorms were in the forecast once again, not only for Pittsburgh, but for Cleveland, too. Today's schedule isn't as tight as yesterdays but we had a much further drive between the two parks today – 2.5 hours, instead of just the 45-minute drive we had yesterday. We'll just have to take it as it comes again and all we can do is hope that we still have some luck left on our side… hopefully we didn't use it all up last night. "Grip it and rip it," as Joey would say.

Once again, as we entered through the gates, we saw the tarp on the field for the second day in a row. This was becoming an all-too-familiar sight.

12:45pm

In our seats with lunch – some sandwiches from Primanti Bros. and an Iron City Beer. We had our picture taken by a photographer from the newspaper already and were now just waiting on Brian.

"When's he meeting us?" asked Pedro.

"Top of the fifth I think he said?" Our seats are top level but right behind home plate so we get the full panoramic scene of the river, its yellow bridges, and the skyline that is all perfectly framed by the ballpark.

"This sandwich is good but the beer… I dunno," Joey said.

I agree. The sandwich has roast beef, French fries and coleslaw on it – something a little different – and it was tasty. But the beer… yeah, I don't know.

"It tastes almost metallic. Like they *actually used* iron as an ingredient," Joey said.

It's been trying to rain but so far it's only been like a light mist. The grounds crew is on the field now clearing the tarp for a punctual start to the game.

2:15pm

"I grew up going to the Vet in Philly," I told Brian, a loyal Pirates fan. "Actually, I was just reminded of the Vet walking through the tunnel to our seats here. The Vet had those small, closed, concrete hallways just like here that lead you to your seats. I remember stepping out at the end of those tunnels and feeling like I stepped into another world.

We continued to talk to Brian about how the Trip started, how we planned it, why we're doing it. We told him that we are most looking forward to seeing the country but are most dreading the long drives and sleepless nights.

4:15pm

The Pirates beat the Marlins 7-4 today for Brian and his undying loyalty to the team.

"Check it out tomorrow, guys. The article will be posted online," Brian said before taking off.

"Thanks, Brian," I said shaking his hand. "Appreciate you taking the time."

As we were leaving, the thermometer hit 42 – the highest its hit all day – and it was windy as shit… not really baseball weather. But we had one game down today and one to go, so I'm not complaining.

71

We were somewhere on the Ohio Turnpike when Joey starting reading an article he found on the internet. "Yo, get this – the Phillies and the Yankees were both rained out the day *after* we were there and then the Red Sox game was rained out the day *before* we were there." He looks up and does a little laugh in disbelief then raises his eyebrows.

"Someone's on our side, man," he said.

We rolled into Cleveland and parked in a garage just outside Progressive Field. (Or, as the locals still call it – Jacobs). Thirty minutes till game time and storm clouds were rolling in.

One of the Indian's signature foods is a type of mustard that's called Bertman's Ballpark Mustard... so I guess it's not technically a food, it's more of a condiment, which I don't think are foods.

"Are condiments considered food?" I ask as I load up my hot dog with the Mustard.

"No," Joey says like that's an idiotic thing to ask. "You don't snack on a bottle of ketchup, do you?"

Good point.

I bit into the Bertman's-loaded hot dog. It was good... tasted like mustard but had a bit of a tang to it in the end... a little kick to it.

"It's good," Pedro said, chewing like a cow on grass.

In our seats, the rain is falling. There is nobody here on this cold, wet night so we took the liberty of moving to seats under a roof. The 10,000 fans at PNC earlier today looked like a sell-out compared to this.

"You look like the Grim Reaper," Joey tells Pedro who has the black hood of his sweatshirt over his head and pulled down over his face. Joey laughs. "You look like the Grim Reaper!"

"I'm cold. My Dominican blood can't handle this," Pedro says.

It was a pitching duel at Progressive (sorry Cleveland – at *Jacobs* tonight) between Cliff Lee and Brian Bannister of the visiting Royals. Despite Lee's 8-inning gem, he was out-dueled and the Indians lost 2-0 on a night that provided a steady, soaking rain.

By the time we got back to the Vanbino, my clothes were drenched so I changed before heading out for Toronto. Tonight, we'd follow I-90 up along the coast of Lake Erie and stop somewhere just south of Niagara Falls so we can see them tomorrow.

The first five days of the Trip were absolutely crazy – we've already visited eight ballparks, driven close to 2,000 miles, lost one of our guys, and have been dealing with cold, rainy weather every day – and I feel like I'm in a daze. My motor is running purely on adrenaline right now.

We're cold, we're wet, and we're tired beyond measure and we figured we owed ourselves a bed with a nice pillow for a change.

3:00am

Joey ended up stopping at a Super 8 Hotel in Buffalo. I don't know what the outside temp was but it was *cold*. Pedro grabbed his bag and ran inside – he was miserable.

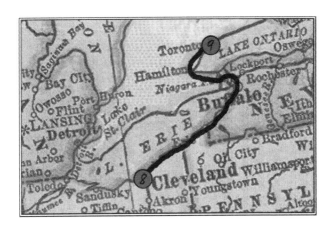

11:00am

Got to sleep in today. BEST. BED. EVER!

We're only two hours from the Rogers Centre with six hours till first pitch, so we had a bit of time to relax and do some sightseeing at the Falls.

"You ever seen the Falls before?" I asked Pedro as he searched in the empty beef jerky bag for any scraps.

"No, never have."

"You ever seen a grown man naked?" Joey asked, quoting a line from one of his favorite movies "Airplane!"

75

"Can't say no to that," he answered after a moment of hesitation. He finally found a piece of jerky and threw it in his mouth.

After a nice, hearty Denny's breakfast, we walked over to the Falls. (By the way, I discovered Pancake Poppers today, which are golden brown balls of hot, fried dough that you dip in warm syrup. I highly recommend next time you find yourself at Denny's).

Before we left for the Trip, while we were packing the Vanbino, Joey clipped a silver ornament of an angel onto the visor above the drivers seat. He never said anything about it but I was curious so I finally asked him what it is.

"She's my guardian angel... she'll keep us safe." Aside from the growing roar of the Falls, there was a long stretch of silence. Rarely was Joey left without something to say.

"I was in a really bad car accident in high school – 11th grade – and, you know, the roads up there in the Poconos are whacked – they're all so narrow and winding and you're going up and down these hills... and at night, it's dark. I mean, so dark you can't see 10 feet in front of you. I was on my way home from a friend's graduation party one night and next thing I knew I was laying in a hospital. It was bad, man. I saw pictures of my car and it was literally half up in a tree and the whole front was just flat." He shakes his head. "Somehow I made it out with nothing too serious – I mean, not even a broken bone. My mom gave me that angel after and told me that 'someone's watching over you.' So I brought the angel with us. Thought it might keep us safe on the road."

By now, we were standing on the edge of the walkway watching the powerful water rush over the cliffs. A heavy mist sat in the air over the water and I could see a rainbow stretching over the Horseshoe Falls. As much as I love watching a game at the ballpark, sightseeing at Niagara was a nice change of pace.

6:00pm

Our first dome came north of the border in Toronto at the Rogers Centre where the Blue Jays call home. I've never been a big fan of baseball in a dome – with the artificial turf and the covered sky – but this park is nice. There's a hotel in the outfield and the roof can partially open so I guess it's not a true dome.

Joey found the signature food that he has to eat here. "Het-dag heyah!" he yelled in his hotdog vendor voice. It never fails to get some passers-by attention.

"Alright! Here with the loaded foot-long," Joey says looking down at it. It's smothered in a giant heap of fried onions and peppers and it's definitely longer than a foot and it's got to have a girth of at least an inch or two. This thing is massive and I can tell by the look in his eye and his speechlessness that the foot-long is intimidating him. "And it's pretty loaded, all right…"

He needed two hands to lift it up to his mouth and it sagged in the middle from the weight as he took his first bite.

6:10pm

Joey's only about halfway through the meal and he's slowing down.

"You don't have to finish, man," I tell him.

"I have to," he says. He chugs half a bottle of PowerAde and continues.

6:20pm

He looks out over the field at the grounds crew prepping the field, leaning against the table. He's in a daze, looks sick, is breathing heavy and there are tiny beads of sweat dotting his forehead. A quarter of the evil hot dog still sits on the paper plate beside him, taunting him, laughing maniacally into his defeated, blank stare.

6:25pm

"Alright, asshole," Joey says to the hot dog, picking up the last couple of bites. This challenge has become personal.

He stuffed the last of it into his mouth and swallowed it without really even chewing it – kind of like how a snake lets a meal just slide down its gullet. He chugged the rest of his cherry PowerAde and gripped at his shirt above his heart.

"Oh, Mother-of-God…" he says looking bloated and sickly. "Done… I did it. Jesus. Porcelain pony's gonna get a workout tonight."

One thing that we really wanted to have happen on this trip was to appear on the big Fan-O-Vision screens that they have at the ballparks. We figured with seeing 30 games in 30 days, our chances would be good but to increase our chances, we made a sign to bring into each ballpark with us. Our sign is a big piece of poster board that says how many ballparks we've been to and how many we have left. Before every game, we tape on the appropriate numbers that we pre-made before the Trip and today I was the one who changed the numbers.

"Dude, what is 9 plus 22?" Pedro asks me as we sit in our seats.

I think for a brief second. "31," I answer. He turns around our sign and stares at me with a huge smile.

'9 Ballparks Down, 22 Ballparks To Go' it says.

I shook my head. "I went to art school, man, what do ya expect?" I secretly hoped that everyone around me was as math-impaired as I was.

9:15pm

We got to talking to some Jays fans a few rows in back of us – a couple, both born and raised in Canada. When they heard that we were from Philly, they were quick to bring up '93 and were telling us all about Carter's Corner out there in left.

"Don't remember '93 very well," Joey said obviously with some bitter resentment.

"I thought you guys are seeing 30..." one of the Jays fans says, studying our 30in30 poster board sign. Uh oh, here it comes.

"Yeah, we are..."

"What's the extra park?" He looks up at me.

I can't get away with one, huh?

10:45pm

Departing Toronto with a nine-hour drive to Cincinnati ahead of us. This time we'd follow along the *north* shore of Lake Erie till we hit Michigan, enter back into the States through Detroit, then continue on south through Ohio.

Unlike the pitching duel from the night before, tonight's game was all offense, with six of the game's seven runs coming off the long ball. The Blue Jays beat Millwood and the Rangers 5-2 and now lead the Majors with 12 wins.

Joey's at the wheel. Good thing he works nights and is used to being awake at this time because 10pm is pretty much past Pedro's bedtime and I'm only good until about midnight.

4:15am

Pulled into a rest stop somewhere around Toledo to get some shut-eye. A little over an hour ago we crossed the Ambassador Bridge that took us into Detroit. There was a whole bunch of detours that the Babe couldn't compute and we ended up getting lost in a scary, run-down neighborhood... but we found our way back to the beaten track and lived to see another day.

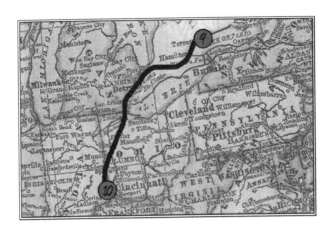

Friday, April 24 — DAY 7
Cincinnati
7:35 Game @ Great American Ballpark (Ballpark #10)
Total Miles Today — 505
Total Miles So Far — 2,273

10:15am

Breakfast today was a breakfast of champions –
honey buns and bear claws from the rest stop vending
machine. It wasn't nearly as gourmet as Denny's but it'll do
just fine.

And, before setting back out on the road, we needed
to do a little Spring Cleaning. With three grown men living
out of her, the Vanbino gets pretty filthy, pretty fast. My
mom would be proud that I'm actually taking the initiative to
clean so this one's for you ma!

We gutted her, piles of our belongings strewn all over the parking spaces on either side of us. We filled a trash bag full of crumpled fast food wrappers, old coffee cups, water bottles, and energy drink cans, swept out the bits of lost jerky and chewed sunflower seeds, and we finally wiped off the glob of dried ketchup on the glove compartment door. I found my little digital camera that I lost three days ago and Joey found his phone charger – whoo-hoo! We separated our dirty clothes from our clean clothes and put everything back in its proper place. (Speaking of dirty clothes and clean clothes – I'm not quite sure when laundry is going to get done and I'm running out of clean clothes. Laundry was a little detail I overlooked when planning the Trip. I might have to pull out one of my old tricks from my college days and start turning my underwear inside-out).

"I've been doing that wash and fold..." Joey starts.

Pedro looks up at him with a quizzical look. "Huh?"

"You know, where you drop off a basket of laundry and they wash it and fold it for you?"

"Oh, nice," Pedro nods.

"Yeah, but I swear every time I get my laundry back I'm missing a pair of underwear. How do I go in there and bring that up? Can you imagine how awkward that conversation would be?"

"That would be awkward," Pedro agreed.

We emptied a bottle of Meadows and Rain scented Febreze and got back into the Vanbino. She was as good as new. Back in business.

2:20pm

We're on I-75, about 45 minutes north of Cincinnati, and we're stuck in our first traffic jam. The game is not until seven so we have plenty of time but we've moved about two feet in the last 20 minutes... and we're stopped dead right now.

2:45pm

The numbers on the clock have changed but the mile markers have not. Still stopped dead...

3:10pm

We finally passed the accident on the left hand side of the road. Two cars were blocking the fast lane, both completely demolished. An ambulance passed us on the shoulder about 30 minutes ago and now it's gone. I hope everyone is okay.

Traffic was funneling into the one far right lane and as we passed the wreckage, I glanced up at Joey's guardian angel.

4:15pm

We hadn't had anything to eat since our honey buns and bear claws so we got some chicken wings and cheeseburgers at the In Between Tavern before heading into the ballpark. (The In Between Tavern – named so because it sits in between Paul Brown Stadium and Great American Ballpark.)

Great American Ballpark sits on the banks of the Ohio River, a river that starts in Pittsburgh at the mouth of the Allegheny where we had ridden that water taxi down to PNC. It's weird but the water taxi ride seems like it happened weeks ago but it's been just a few days.

To kill a bit of time, we walked down Pete Rose Way and around to the back of the ballpark to get a better view of the river. There's a pretty neat little thing back there called the Steamboat Monument and it's a whole bunch of little towers sticking out of the ground that you can make whistle like a steamboat. Speaking of steamboats, there was one right there on the water and right beyond that, on the other side of the river, is Kentucky.

We found a couple of people down there setting up some huge fireworks.

"You fellas goin' to the game tonight?" asked the guy, probably about 35 years old, wearing thick, heavy work gloves.

"Yeah, are there fireworks tonight?" asked Pedro.

"You bet."

Nice! Fireworks at the ballpark always reminds me of my favorite scene in the Sandlot when they play the one night game of the year on the Fourth of July.

We chatted some more with our firework friend and came to learn a neat little fun fact – 70% of the Ohio River is actually *in Kentucky*.

"So why is it called the *Ohio* River? I don't get it." He seems to direct his question more to the Gods than to us and the apparent frustration behind his words hint at how much he is tortured by it. I felt like I was letting the poor guy down when I came up empty for an answer.

The Skyline Chili Cheese Dogs seem to be pretty popular here so we decided on that for a late dinner. One order is actually three miniature-sized hotdogs and they are smothered in hot chili and grated cheddar cheese. Delicious.

Joey got a local beer called the Nutty Brunette. "I've certainly had a few of these in my life," he said as he hoisted his cup in the air for a toast. "Both have a little bit of bite."

The Reds are hosting the Braves tonight and I guess there's some tension between these two teams because the benches cleared at one point after Volquez hit a batter.

"Lotta babes here," Joey said looking at a group of girls walking to their seats. "I gotta come back. Nice park, too."

Just beyond the steamboat in center field, the fireworks lit up the night sky in brilliant colors. Pedro and I reclined in our seats; Joey danced to the Frank Sinatra soundtrack in the aisles. One of those glistening white fireworks with the long streamers just burst and now hung in the air while some green and red ones pop around it. The reflection in the Kentucky... eh-hem, I mean the *Ohio* River is beautiful.

Great American Ballpark is already Ballpark #10 for us, and, only a week into the Trip, we already had a third of the ballparks completed. Elvis came on and "Hound Dog" echoed throughout the ballpark. I looked back at Joey and he was in his element – he loves Elvis. He wants to stop at Graceland if we have a chance.

"I'm not driving 20,000 miles and not going to Graceland," he said.

After 10 ballparks, we've hit our stride and we're finding a routine. We've found that it's best to drive most of the distance to the next city overnight so that way we'd only have two hours tops to get to the ballpark. We'd get to the city as soon as we could so if we did end up hitting any traffic or having any car troubles, we'd at least be close by and less likely to miss the game. The Vanbino was becoming more comfortable by the day and the road was becoming... well, *soothing*, actually... and familiar.

The fireworks finished in a grand flurry of exploding light and color. I don't know what it is about baseball and fireworks but they just *go* together, like peanut butter and chocolate just *goes* together.

Back at the Vanbino, Pedro offered to drive as we packed some things up.

"Chi-town tomorrow. Little sausage, little deep dish... bada-bing!" Joey said. Tomorrow would be our first of two trips we'd have to make to the Windy City. The Cubs and White Sox were never home at the same time during the Trip but we'd be back up around the Great Lakes next week for the Twins, Brewers, and Tigers so we'll stop into Wrigley then.

On the road again.

The subtle hum of the engine hang softly in the background and the soft vibrations from the running motor and the grooves in the road lull me to sleep, my eyes growing heavy. Pedro has some Johnny Cash playing through the stereo. It's been a long time since I listened to Johnny and, wow... he really sounds good tonight. There's something mesmerizing about listening to a Johnny track while driving on the open road... I don't know... the two just seem to go together, like... well, like fireworks and baseball.

We're two hours from Chicago and decided to get a hotel tonight. An older lady worked the front desk at this Motel 6 and when she looked at Joey's PA license, she asked "what brings you boys all the way out here?"

"We're just taking a little road trip," Joey answered. "We're driving across the country to see some ballparks."

Silence as she typed some stuff up in her computer. "Good for you guys. I miss out on a lot of sleep during this shift but I don't care – it gives me the opportunity to do a lot more. If you have the opportunity to do something, I say do it. That way you can never look back and wonder what you missed." She has wild black hair that she had attempted to pull back in a bun but clumps stick out in all directions. Her large glasses sit down low on her nose, just above the tip, and as she types she has to tilt her head so her eyes can see above the thick rims. She is dressed all in black, and as she speaks, her head bobs all around like a bobble head and she sucks on a piece of hard candy. "You only come this way once and I don't wanna miss out on nuthin! ...I always say I can sleep when I'm dead."

With her wild, frayed black hair and her saggy eyes, I thought she seemed a little whacked... especially when she first started talking. But I thought about what she said and I took it to heart. There's truth in her words and I know, no matter what the outcome is of this Trip, I won't regret having done it because an opportunity presented itself and we seized it.

I can sleep when I'm dead.

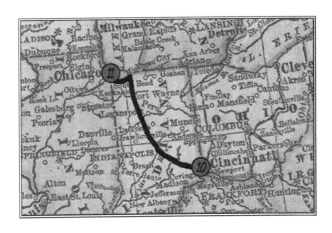

10:00am

We had a nice breakfast at a Cracker Barrel earlier and now are hanging around our room till checkout. I love the Vanbino, I do… but it is *so nice* to be able to stretch out!

The Weather Channel is not telling us what we want to hear. Today's forecast for Chicago is gloomy – severe thunderstorms right around game time. And it gets worse – for the next week, the mid-western states are under severe thunderstorm and tornado watches. This includes cities as north as Chicago and as south as Dallas, St. Louis, Kansas City, and everywhere in between. Oh, and guess what?

Those four cities I just mentioned just happen to be the next four days of our Trip.

"We may have to forget about a ballpark chasing documentary and turn this into a storm chasing one," I say.

1:30pm

Lake Shore Drive snakes along the western banks of the enormous Lake Michigan, passing the Field Museum, Soldier Field, and dumping us off into downtown Chicago. I was here once before but it was brief and today I was looking forward to a little sightseeing. The skies are sunny and it is a beautiful day out right now! But it's still early and this is exactly what happened that day in Baltimore. Baltimore! Jeez... was that really less than a week ago?? For some weird reason it seems like months ago.

Millennium Park was bustling – people everywhere! Couples and kids playing in the fountains, artists painting the scenes, street bands playing their songs; everybody was out today. We took some pictures at the Bean and at the Gardens then found a little pizza joint and got some deep-dish. Joey had been talking about deep-dish pizza since the beginning of the Trip and now here he is, face to face with it.

"Not bad," he said with a piece of sausage falling from the corner of his mouth.

Then we heard the thunder.

While inside the pizza parlor, the skies had darkened considerably and thunder now rolled off in the distance. The Vanbino was parked five blocks away so we didn't waste anytime settling up and getting out of there. We were about a block from the Vanbino when it started raining, and I mean HARD! Torrential rain. We sprinted the rest of the way but it didn't do much good – we were soaked by the time we got there.

"Why didn't we bring umbrellas?" I asked.

"I dunno. We're whacked," Joey said.

5:30pm

By the time we reached U.S. Cellular Field, the rain was much lighter but out past the Sears Tower, lightning streaked across the sky. It was cold outside, too – 52 degrees but the heavy wind made it feel a lot colder. A tailgate invited us in and we shot-gunned some beers and ate some grilled-in-the-husk corn-on-the-cob with them to stay warm. This group is die-hard Sox fans and they treated us like old friends they hadn't seen in years.

"I never saw anybody grill their corn on the cob," I say to Colin who's celebrating his birthday today. "Is that a Chicago thing?"

"I dunno," he says. "I've always done it. You have to make sure to grill it in the husk to trap in all the juices and flavors."

Before heading into the ballpark, we took a walk around to Gate 5 where a plaque sits to commemorate the old Comiskey Park. I wanted to try and see as many old ballpark sites as we could along the way because this was a trip for the ballpark, after all. I stepped up to the home plate-shaped plaque that sits in the parking lot of Gate 5.

"Comiskey Park, 1910-1990"

This park was loved. This park, like Yankee
Stadium, like Shea, had charm and it was loved by its fans
like a family loves their home. The White Sox faithful (just
like the fans in Cleveland) refuse to call their new park by its
name, opting instead to keep the name Comiskey alive.

9:00pm

The Blue Jays followed us down to Chicago and are
currently being routed by Mark Buehrle and his offense.
The Sox are up 10-2 right now, powered by a grand slam off
the bat of Alexei Ramirez.

"Pedro missed it!" I said to Joey. It is now the 7th
inning and Pedro has been missing since the 4th.

"That's what happens when you go to Fire Island,"
Joey told me. Pedro has seemed distant these last couple of
days. I wonder if something's up.

"I'll tell ya what, I could use a little Fire Island up
here. It's freezing," Joey said. It really is cold. I'm bundled
up in all my winter gear but the wind is still slipping in
through the cracks.

1:00am

We're on I-55 south. Destination – St. Louis.
Tomorrow is a 1:05 game at Busch Stadium against the rival
Cubs. Aside from the constant threat of rain, the next couple
of days should be pretty mellow. After our afternoon game

tomorrow, our next game isn't until 7:00 in Kansas City – just a four hour drive from St. Louis.

Pedro is behind the wheel. He has a bag of sunflower seeds in one hand and an empty McDonald's cup in the other. "Walk the Line" plays faintly on the stereo and I notice his head is not bopping to the beat. He loves this song and he usually sings along with it. Instead, he stares straight ahead; chews a seed then spits, chews then spits.

"Let me get some seeds?" I ask Pedro from the passenger seat. He pours some into my outstretched hand. "How you doing? You alright?"

He nods slightly, unconvincingly. Then he shrugs and shakes his head. Chews on a seed. "Krystal and I are in a little bit of a thing," he confesses. "I just… uh… it's hard being away from her. Especially since our schedules are so opposite. I call her and she's busy. She calls me and I'm busy. I feel like I haven't *talked* to her since I left." He spits out the shell. I notice it misses the cup but I don't say anything. It sticks to the dashboard… it's okay. I'll get it later.

"You guys are out of sync, that's all," I tell him. I was talking out of my ass – I don't know anything about long distance relationships. Out of sync? That didn't sound too bad so I went with it. "It happens. You just gotta make time, ya know? You both gotta make time. Like a date. Like a phone date. You just gotta get back in sync with each other and you'll be fine."

Pedro nodded as he threw another handful of seeds into his mouth and chewed them like a cow. The secret to beating road fatigue, by the way, is eating sunflower seeds. Trust me on this one. It works amazingly well.

Sunday, April 26 — DAY 9
St. Louis
1:05 Game @ Busch Stadium (Ballpark #12)
Total Miles Today — 297
Total Miles So Far — 2,865

11:30am

 We woke up to sunny skies and 65 degrees. If the weather holds, today will be a good day.

 Since we set out, I've been getting a lot of emails from people all over the country who've heard about our trip and they share ballpark road trips that they have taken. One of those emails was from Brent and Carrie, a couple who live outside St. Louis with their two kids, and they invited us to tailgate with them before the game today. So we got to the park early today and when we pulled into the parking lot beside Busch, we found Brent and Carrie right away.

97

"Great to meet you guys!" Carrie said greeting us with a hug. Brent greeted us by putting a hot brat and a cold Stag in each of our hands.

"You come to St. Louis, you drink a Stag," he said snapping open a pounder can of his own.

Carrie, having rounded up her two young kids, introduced them. "This is Montana and this is little Clarkey," she said putting her hand on her three-year-old son's head.

"Can you tell we're 49er fans?" Brent said with a laugh.

This was a family of sports fanatics and they don't just visit ballparks – they visit football stadiums, hockey and basketball arenas, and not just pro, but college, too. They're serious. Ballpark chasers are fans of the game first and foremost, but it's the actual ballpark experience that drive them all over the country. Brent, Carrie and their two kids are the epitome of ballpark chasing.

"So Montana has four ballparks left to see and Clarkey has twelve... we figured we could drop them off with you guys so they can finish them up?" Carrie said laughing.

"Of course!" I said. "We have plenty of room in the car-top carrier." Montana didn't like that idea but her younger brother Clark thought it sounded awesome.

We said our good-byes then headed on to get our tickets but because it was a Sunday day game and it was against the rival Cubbies, we had a tough time getting them. We eventually managed to find some standing room only.

We were in Dizzy's Diner on the third base side of Busch eating fried ravioli when we met Tom, Christian, and Doug. We noticed them looking out over the empty lot across the street, pointing and talking. I had a hunch of what was once on that lot so I went up to them and introduced myself.

"That is the sacred grounds of St. Louis Cardinals baseball..." Christian looked out over the empty field of grass, "...awesome! *Best* times of my life." He spoke with conviction and love that one would use to speak of a close friend or family member. It was apparent that old ballpark meant a lot to him.

Tom spoke and he, too, looked out over the empty field. That field is empty in my eyes but not in theirs – I think they can still see the ghost of the old ballpark standing over there. "We had a lot of good times over there, drank a lot of beer, had a lot of laughs..." he laughs and turns to me. "We were the *definition* of bleacher bums."

"I was up on that roof there," Doug started, pointing to a parking garage on the other side of the lot, "and I saw the wrecking ball drop and knock down the first Busch. It was emotional... it was weird, really. I felt like I was losing a part of my childhood or something."

"There was a lot of tradition over there," Tom chimed, "a *lot* of tradition. Not so much over here now, but this park is still new and we're trying to renew it."

The Cubs crushed the Cards today 10-3 thanks to a home run and a five RBI performance from Fukudome on his birthday.

Right now, we're on our way to this cool little bar we happened to pass earlier this morning. We just had dinner with Carrie and Brent at Schlafly's Tap Room, a local brewery and grill here in downtown St. Louis. I had the Tap Room Burger – a sirloin burger with coleslaw on an English muffin. It's probably one of the best burgers I've ever had.

But the Oyster Bar, where we're headed now, looks like the place to be. It is a shanty little shack of a bar on the corner of Broadway and Gratiot Street, just a few blocks from Busch. From the outside, it looks like a shit-hole... but a shit-hole that has the potential to be awesome.

We entered through an opening in the leaning wood fence and walked onto the side patio, which was just a sloping, uneven brick floor. A giant tree grew from the center of the patio and up through the tin-slabbed roof. Lanterns and strings of Christmas lights hang from the low, thick branches of the tree and the beams of the roof and they offer the only light in the dark, covered area. It was packed and after we found a table, I noticed all the Cubs and Cards fans. This must be the place to go after the games.

Tonight would be a good night where we can just relax and hang out and get some drinks. We're going to get a hotel here tonight so we don't have to do *any* driving! That'll be nice for a change.

St. Louis has been a literal feast – first the tailgate, then we got foot-long corndogs, then foot-long brats, and then fried raviolis in Busch, then the burgers at Schlafly's, and now some oysters and a bucket of crawfish at the Oyster Bar. I definitely gained some weight today and I'm sure my cholesterol isn't ideal right now either... come to think of it, I don't think I've had one piece of fruit or vegetable this whole trip yet. These first nine days have been nothing but beer, coffee, fried shit at the ballpark, and fast food on the road.

But if it sounds like I'm complaining, I'm not. I love fried shit and beer.

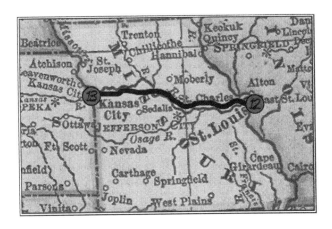

Monday, April 27 — DAY 10
Kansas City
7:05 Game @ Kauffman Stadium (Ballpark #13)
Total Miles Today — 248
Total Miles So Far — 3,113

11:20am

 I don't know if it's the hangover or the lack of nutrients in my body, but I feel like crap this morning. Joey and I let loose last night (Oyster Bar is just an awesome, *awesome* time) but thank God for Pedro, always the responsible one, who got us safely to a Comfort Inn. (Speaking of which – the free breakfast at the Comfort Inn is worth the price of the room alone. They have a waffle bar, okay? Enough said.)

 Today, we're starting with some sightseeing at the Arch.

The iconic Arch in St. Louis sits on the western bank of the Mighty Mississippi, built in the early 60's as a tribute to the pioneers of westward expansion and now stands as a symbol to the gateway to the west. Standing underneath it looking up, the stainless steel skin of the Arch reflecting the sunlight so well and its symmetry so perfect, I can only describe it as majestic. It didn't look nearly this big from the ballpark yesterday and I was surprised to learn that it is the tallest memorial in the U.S.

We boarded our little car that climbs up one leg of the Arch. It's tiny, round, and is supported on just a hinge so it swings back and forth as it ascends and descends the Arch.

"It's like a space capsule... they're gonna blast us to Mars," Joey said as he climbed in through the tiny door. "It's gonna be ten years in the future when we come back down and we'll have no idea what happened." He bit into a stick of buffalo jerky he got at the gift shop.

"Can I have a bite?" I asked.

I took a bite and handed it back. "Not bad."

Our ship docked at the top and the little hatch door opened. The first thing I saw when I looked out the window was Busch Stadium, sitting 630 feet below me, looking like a model toy. Then I saw the Vanbino looking like a Micro-Machine and then the Mighty Miss, stretching in both directions for as far as my eye could see. You can also feel the Arch sway in the wind, which is a bit unnerving at first, but after a while, you don't even notice it.

12:50pm

The skies are heavily clouded and it's nice and cool out right now. Severe thunderstorms are still forecast for the Midwest, including tonight in Kansas City. Before leaving town, we had a catch in the park under the Arch. We liked it here – it's a nice town, with great people and incredible food.

3:30pm

Driving west on I-70 across Missouri, the floodgates opened. I mean, literally, one second there was no rain and the next it was teeming rain where we couldn't even see out the windshield. Hopefully this would be the worst of it. Kauffman is Ballpark #13, however… and I'm superstitious.

5:00pm

We're only 10 minutes from Kauffman Stadium and we're at the Auto Center at a local Wal-Mart. Nothing serious – we just want to get an oil change and tune-up since we have some time to spare. We've clocked just over 3,000 miles so far but we have two big drives coming up in the next couple of days – tonight, 600 miles to Arlington, TX, then tomorrow, 1,000 miles to Minneapolis.

5:45pm

I really wanted some KC barbeque while we were in town and wouldn't you know it but by sheer luck, when we pulled in and parked at Kauffman, we just happened to be next to the manager of a restaurant called Jacks Stacks BBQ who was tailgating with some friends. We hung out for a while but before going in, he called his restaurant and told them that "some baseball guys" are stopping by after the game tonight. He gave us a gift card and told us to get the burnt ends.

"Burnt ends?" I asked.

"Just trust me," he replied with a half smile.

What are the chances of parking next to the manager of a barbeque joint?? Talk about luck. By the time we got into the ballpark, the rain had fizzled to nothing more than a light mist.

"Somebody's on our side, ya know?" Joey said. "Another cold, rainy day but we're getting the game in."

"Lucky 13," I said.

Because it was so cold and wet, Kauffman was empty (attendance numbers not even reaching 10,000) and we got to sit pretty close to the field behind home plate. Our old friends, the Toronto Blue Jays, followed us into town once again. Bannister pitched again and he was dominant just like when we saw him in Cleveland. I sat there in my winter jacket and snow hat, shivering. Grim Reaper Pedro and his Dominican blood were doing the same.

"I need to move, man. I'm too cold," he said and we all got up. There was a lot to see here at this ballpark anyway. Kaufman opened in '73, the one bright spot in an otherwise Dark Age of ballpark design. The team just put $60 million of renovations into this place before the season opened and the entire park – from the enormous digital scoreboard to the fountains in the outfield – looks amazing.

They did a great job here preserving the charm of the original Kauffman while updating its amenities.

We were on our way to the outfield to check out the fountains when we came across a vendor that was selling rib-eye steak sandwiches. Are you kidding me?? I wanted to save room for the barbeque later tonight but how could I pass up a rib-eye steak sandwich?? I got one… and so glad I did because it was hands down one of the best meals I've had so far… not just on the Trip so far, but so far in my life! A rib-eye steak with some lettuce, a tomato, an onion ring, and some sauce – bliss on a bun.

10:20pm

They were waiting for us when we rolled into Jacks Stacks.

"You the baseball boys, huh?" the manager asked.

"Yeah, that's us." They sat us, and along with the menus, brought us out an enormous cut of barbequed prime rib "our specialty… on the house" the waiter said.

11:15pm

After being treated like royalty, I sat reclined in the booth, hardly able to move, not wanting to leave. The ribs and the chicken and the beans and potatoes and the burnt ends, oh man, the burnt ends! They come from the point ends of the brisket but are re-seasoned and are cooked longer, making these bite-sized morsels more tender and more flavorful. Between the rib-eye steak sandwich from

Kauffman and the barbeque, I now know what heaven tastes like.

We rode 71 south along the Kansas-Missouri border and when we hit Joplin, jumped onto 44 towards Tulsa. I'm parked at a rest stop in Muskogee, Oklahoma. We're still 4.5 hours from Arlington but I'm half asleep at the wheel and can't drive anymore.

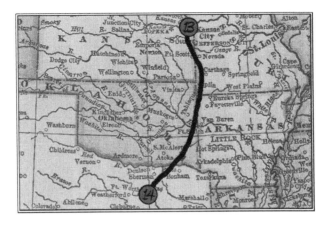

10:30am

Another comfortable night in the Vanbino…

I freshened up a bit in the bathroom – brushed my teeth, put on a fresh layer of deodorant, a clean shirt… when was the last time I showered? Oh, yeah, it was just last night in St. Louis. That's not bad – more recent than I thought. But the laundry is becoming a serious situation. I don't really know what's clean and what's dirty anymore because the dirty shirts are smelling up the clean shirts so I can no longer go by smell.

Pedro was the one behind the wheel when the blue and red lights started flashing through the Vanbino.

"Oh, shit. Is that for me?" Pedro asked looking at the cop car tailing him in the rearview mirror.

"Probably," I said. "You were going pretty fast." For the first week or so of the Trip, Pedro had Joey and I white-knuckled whenever he was in the driver's seat but since the Baltimore-to-DC roller coaster ride he took us on, we've grown accustomed to his driving "style" (I guess you can call it).

"You know the limit here?" the officer asked as Pedro handed him his license.

"80?" he guessed.

"70," the officer said looking at the license. "You know how fast *you* were going?

"75?"

The officer looked up. "92."

Joey and I had a bet going who would get the first ticket – I had Joey and Joey had Pedro. I looked back at Joey from the front passenger seat and he was looking at me, a little smirk on one side of his mouth, rubbing his thumb and pointer finger together telling me to pay up.

We're in Dealey Plaza right now in downtown Dallas and I am writing this entry from behind the wooden fence on the grassy knoll. The back of the fence is covered in graffiti of messages, poems, and doodles to JFK. Just ahead of me is the paint on the road that marks his fatal head-shot, and to my left, the Book Depository. It's eerie here. There's a heavy, almost unnatural, silence hanging in the air.

We left and drove down Elm Street and under the overpass to get to Sherlock's.

5:00pm

An article had been written up about us in the Dallas-Fort Worth newspaper. Some locals had read it and they contacted us to meet up before the game. We decided on Sherlock's Pub because they have a complimentary bus service to and from the ballpark. (Any chance we can get to save on gas and parking, we'll take).

Ralph and Royce, ballpark chasers in their own right, met us at Sherlock's Pub.

Ralph, an older man who retired in Dallas, is actually from Manayunk (a town just outside Philadelphia) and he is a Phillies fan. He pulled out a picture of him, Harry Kalas, and Richie Ashburn on a golf course.

"Talk about luck!" Ralph beamed. "I just show up at my golf course one day and next thing you know I'm hittin' the greens with Whitey and Harry! It was a day I won't ever forget."

"How were they?" Joey asked.

He laughed. "You know, to be honest with you, I don't even remember how they shot. I just remember them bein' a couple a great guys. Lots of fun, you know? Very personable. Very funny guys," he said looking at his treasured picture.

For two hours, we swapped baseball stories and it's a good thing for the complimentary bus we were taking to the ballpark because they were buying us Shiners the whole time.

"Anything you guys need while you're in Texas, you give me a call," Royce said. "I'll be happy to help ya."

"Thanks," I say. "But we'll be on our way to Minnesota tonight."

7:25pm

At the gates of Rangers Ballpark, the guy taking our tickets saw our video camera and asked us what it's for.

"We're doing this road trip – we're seeing all 30 ballparks in 30 days and we're filming it," Pedro explained.

"Are you serious?! That is awesome!" The guy radioed some other guy and he showed us to our new, complimentary seats – 15 rows off the field between third and home! This must be what they mean by southern hospitality!

The outfield of Rangers Ballpark is unique. It is closed (unlike most of the other new parks like PNC or

Busch that offer skyline views) and it is an architectural montage of classic ballparks. The roofed home run porch in right field is reminiscent of Tiger Stadium, the frieze around the top a nod to pre-1973 Yankee Stadium, the out-of-town scoreboard in left (once manual but now digital) a tribute to Fenway, the arched windows a reminder of Comiskey, and the numerous nooks and crannies in the outfield fence a reflection of Ebbets Field.

10:45pm

We saw Kevin Millwood pitch for the second time this trip and unlike his first outing we saw in Toronto, he won today against the A's, 5-4. It was a really good game, back and forth most of the way and the Rangers scored their winning run in the eighth off a Nelson Cruz single to left.

11:10pm

Back at the Vanbino in the Sherlock's parking lot and the first "crazy" drive of the Trip looms ahead. We have a Twins game tomorrow at 7:00 in Minneapolis but there is 961 miles of road and 16 and half hours of driving between us. We'll cut clear across the Great Plains tonight to make our way north to Minnesota.

"Alright! Amp time!" Joey said pulling out two of his 16oz. energy drinks from his stash in the back. He looks at me with a can in each hand. "Possibly the main key to the whole trip."

He snapped one open in the driver's seat and chugged about half of it.

113

"On the road again! Minnesota!" Joey clapped, cued up his iPod, and pulled out of the parking space. "Grip it and rip it. Whatever it takes!"

I woke up and realized we were stopped on the shoulder of the highway. Pedro was passed out in the back, the Vanbino was running, but Joey was missing. I looked out the windows – pitch black. I mean nothing! I was groggy and my vision was blurry but when I say it was dark out there, I mean it was *dark* out there!

This is exactly how horror movies start… a few buddies road tripping across the country, one wakes up in the middle of the night, in the middle of nowhere, only to find his friend has mysteriously disappeared…

…and then Joey's white shirt fades into view and he gets back into the van.

"There is nothing out here. I mean, not shit. I've been holding my breath for an hour I've had to piss so bad but there hasn't been anywhere to stop! If you break down out here, you're screwed, man. They won't find you. It's like Jeepers Creepers out here."

"Where are we?" I muttered.

Merging back onto the highway (which really isn't even a highway, it's more of just a two lane road with a few tractor trailers here and there), Joey thought about it for a minute, " we're on the back roads of hell," he finally answers. "This is creepy out here, man. This is Jeepers Creepers."

114

"Want me to take over for a bit?"

"Nah, I'm good. I'm jamming." He was almost glowing from that neon green liquid Amp coursing through his veins.

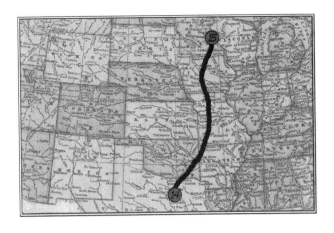

8:30am

I noticed the sun above a flat horizon as I opened my eyes and found myself gazing out the window. I was dazed and confused but I quickly came around.

Joey was still in the driver's seat, hunched forward, his hands gripping 10 and 2 on the wheel. He glanced over at me, his eyes barely open, just slits in his face with big, saggy black bags under them. He looked like a shell of himself, like an alien had snatched him up, hijacked his body, and threw the Joey that we all know and love out for dead. His eyes were empty… soulless even.

"Wakey, wakey…" he uttered to me, sounding a little loopy and not at all like himself.

I looked in the back and Pedro was in the same position as when I last saw him six hours ago. "Dude, you been driving all night??" I asked Joey.

"Yeah, I'm fine, though."

"You look like shit. Pull over, man, I'm gonna take over."

Joey was unresponsive and lifeless, having long since been lulled into a deep trance by the monotony of the straight, dark highway. Nine hours of overnight driving, alone, through the Great Plains will do that to you, I guess.

I felt terrible. "Why didn't you wake me up, man?"

Without moving his lifeless gaze from the road, he said in a weak voice, "I'm in a groove."

"Alright, well pull over and I'll drive. How did you stay awake?"

He finally broke his trance from the road and turned to me with a grin, "two Amps and a double shot espresso from Starbucks that I found in the back."

Yeah, that'll do it.

9:30am

As we crossed into Iowa, Joey parked the Vanbino in a rest stop. We emerged from our mobile home groggy

118

and a bit disoriented, three nomads trying to find their present bearings, still adjusting to a life of constant movement.

The morning was crisp and the fresh air aroused my senses, woke me up a little. A heavy, early morning fog sat just above the grass and I could hear a choir of birds singing from the forest behind the restroom hut.

Pedro walked to the edge of the trees to brush his teeth. He refused to brush them inside rest stop bathrooms at a sink with running water. "Because that's where strangers shit," he said. Fair enough.

I was outside the Vanbino stretching my legs and enjoying the fresh air and Joey was rooting around the trunk of the Vanbino for something.

And that's when I heard it – a violent splattering of fluids against the pavement coming from behind the Vanbino.

I grabbed the camera and ran to the back of the van to find Joey hunched over, hands on knees, head between his legs, breathing heavy and spitting. A pool of chunky and bright, neon green vomit sat between his feet – the green color was from the Amps and the chunks were bits of jerky, no doubt.

"I got frickin' swine flu," Joey says as he frantically digs around the trunk for his Tums. He finally finds them and chugs the bottle as if it were the last bit of crumbs in a bag of Cracker Jack. "No, I'm not sick, it's just all the shit I've been eating. Eating shit, drinking shit... just shit," and he takes another swig of his Tums.

10:15am

By Iowa, the flat plains gradually turned into rolling hills and the landscape became more dotted with farmhouses and silos, cows and horses, and the occasional field of wind turbines.

In the five-hour stretch between Winterset, IA and Minneapolis, we stopped at John Wayne's birthplace and the covered bridges from the Bridges of Madison County movie. Joey loved the Duke's place but he wasn't thrilled with the bridges.

"They're bridges… so what? Big deal. I see bridges all the time."

Pedro loved them.

5:30pm

Surprise, surprise – we were met with rain in Minneapolis but luckily the Twins are still playing in the Metrodome and so we don't have to worry about the weather tonight.

The park wasn't too crowded and we were able to go down and sit just a few rows from the field. Joey had made a miraculous recovery and he somehow consumed two Dome Dogs and a beer.

"I hope you throw up right now," I told him, watching him stuff himself. He was making *me* sick.

There's a big sign in the outfield that has a countdown to outdoor baseball. I definitely prefer outdoor baseball to sitting and watching it being played under a roof but in Minnesota? I don't know... it's going to be pretty cold up here in April and September and even October when the Twins make it into the playoffs. I'm just glad that Target Field is still under construction because if there wasn't a roof over us tonight, we certainly would have been rained out. I can actually hear the heavy rain pounding on the roof of the Metrodome right now.

"So does this mean we have to come back next year to Target Field?" Pedro asked.

"Of course," I told him. "Some of those games are gonna get pretty cold, man. Especially in October."

"I read that it's going to be heated," Joey said.

"Heated?" Pedro wondered.

Joey thought about it for a second. "Yeah. They're installing some kind of advanced heating system in the floors or something. And something with its shape... I think it's designed to hold in heat even though there isn't a roof..."

Pedro looks at him disbelievingly. "Pedro, I dunno. Jesus."

"Dude, look at the bags under your eyes," Pedro points out to Joey with a smile. "You look like shit."

"You know what, Pedro... we can't all be beautiful."

121

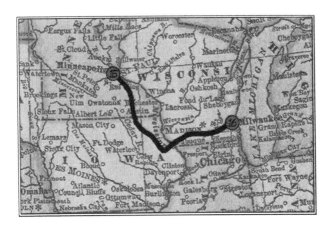

Thursday, April 30 — DAY 13
Milwaukee
7:35 Game @ Miller Park (Ballpark #16)
Total Miles Today — 336
Total Miles So Far — 4,974

8:45am

     Big day ahead of us! Pedro is turning 26 today and Krystal is flying into Milwaukee for the night to help us celebrate.

     "Uh-oh! Fire Island!! Up close and personal!!!" Joey said from the back seat. I looked over at Pedro, laughing. He had the video camera up in front of his face as he filmed some landscape shots but I could see his mouth curve into a smile. He didn't want to encourage Joey so he ignored him.

We were parked in a rest stop for most of the night about two hours southeast of Minneapolis. It's nice being able to park for the night, crack some windows and let the cool northern air into the Vanbino.

Our day today begins in a little town in the middle of Iowa called Dyersville on a famous little baseball field that sits in the middle of cornfields. The Field of Dreams was only three hours out of our way en route to Milwaukee from Minneapolis, but we didn't see it as "out of our way." To us, the Field of Dreams was as much a destination as any one of the other ballparks and so we made our pilgrimage to the holy site with zero hesitation.

The famous ball field sits at the end of a long gravel road and as we drove up to it, the familiar, white farmhouse from the movie came into view, then the tops of the outfield lights, then the top of the metal backstop and then finally we could see the field itself. It sits there, silent and still in the morning mist, welcoming us, calling to us, inviting us onto her pristine, plush, perfect green grass. The field was empty, the bleachers were empty and as I stepped out onto the gravel with my glove and bat in hand, I could feel it. There was something powerful going on here – there was an undeniable energy in the air. Here I stood, in a place I had never been before, a place so new but so familiar.

To explore the Field of Dreams, you need pay no admission, buy no tickets, book no tours. The Field of Dreams is open and free to all. After a little while of playing some ball, a car approached, parked and a man walked towards the field. He was tall and slender with slick-backed Dapper Dan hair and sporty sunglasses, a nice polo on, polished shoes and crisp khakis. He looked like a New York exec... out of place in this small Iowa farming town. He waved to us as he climbed the rickety wooden bleachers and took a seat in the second row from the top. He reclined back and looked off into the distance.

I waved back and we continued to play.

Then, a little while later, a 16-wheeler crept slowly up the gravel road and parked. Another man emerged, dressed in old, weathered denim jeans, a thick flannel shirt and a baseball cap. He, too, waved to us as he made his way to the bleachers and when he reached them he shook hands with the New York exec. Do they know each other? They're talking as if they know each other.

We walked in to the bleachers and introduced ourselves. Formalities didn't last long and after just a few minutes, we were all already old friends.

Felix (the New York exec) has been married for 12 years and has two kids with his wife. Two days ago, she told him she's gay and has been having an affair with another woman for five years.

"She wants a divorce and I don't know what to do now. Everything I thought I knew is just a fabrication." Felix continued in a very relaxed, calm voice, still reclined atop the bleachers, gazing out onto the sun-drenched field. He was quick to share his story with us, something that seemed too personal to share with strangers. But for whatever reason, it wasn't weird, and we didn't feel like strangers.

Ed is a truck driver, probably about 50, 55 or so with white hair and big, callused hands. He and his dad had planned to come here together for the first time five years ago but they never made it – his dad passed away just a month before they were due to come.

"Watching that movie together was our thing and, as corny as it sounds, it was our dream to have a catch here, but uh... never made it." Ed sits near the bottom of the bleachers, and he, too, gazes out onto the field. A slight breeze blew sweeping across the blades of grass and the seedlings of corn in the outfield, and when nobody spoke, the silence was golden.

What's going on here? These people are all strangers and yet they're opening up and sharing stories that are ordinarily reserved for close friends and family – not strangers... not people you just met. And there isn't even hesitation to share; they open up on their own will and it feels completely natural. Somehow, somewhere along that gravel road, judgment is shed and left at the curb. There is no room for that here. This is a place people come seeking serenity and they find it and though you may never see Shoeless Joe here, this is a place where dreams can, and do, come true. This tiny little patch in the middle of an Iowa cornfield is hallowed ground. It is a mecca, not necessarily to the *sport* of baseball, but to the *power* of baseball and the unique way in which it binds us. I've never experienced anything quite like this before.

Is this heaven? If not, it's pretty close.

"What a way to start my birthday," Pedro says to no one in particular. Before leaving, Felix and Ed joined us for a little game of ball on the field. We gave Ed a glove and had a catch with him; it wasn't a catch with his dad but the smile on his face proved that he was content.

Pedro sat in the front seat as we pulled up to the valet podium of the Ambassador Hotel. He looked out the window for Krystal, smiling like a little boy sitting in front of his pile of presents on Christmas morning just before digging in. Pedro told me earlier that this had been the longest he had gone without seeing Krystal in the four years that they've been dating.

The front doors of the hotel slid open and Krystal dashed through them. Pedro jumped out and they embraced. It was the happiest I've seen him the whole trip.

"Fire Island," Joey said to me. "Hope you're ready for this shit."

"This is too much, Krystal," I told her as we walked through our room. This wasn't any old hotel room that Krystal had treated us to tonight – this was the Presidential Suite! And it certainly lived up to its name. Not only are there couches in this Presidential Suite but there's a hot tub... *and* there's stairs. I mean, stairs! In the hotel room! This was the biggest hotel room I've ever been in. We're living large tonight, baby! Joey was excited, too, until he read something online about the hotel.

"Dude, apparently Jeffrey Dahmer stayed at this place in one of the suites..." he said with frightened wide eyes. "There's only two suites here and we're in one..."

"I heard he ate people here," Pedro added to egg Joey on.

"This isn't good. There's spooks here. I'm not gonna be able to sleep tonight..." Joey said.

"You'll be fine, man. Wanna sleep in shifts?" I asked him, joking.

He looks up at me from his computer and, completely serious, says, "that's probably a good idea."

Krystal ordered up some craft brews to the room and we had a little birthday celebration with some cake before heading out. Milwaukee has a lot of food I want to try and so before the ballpark, we're stopping at Solly's for dinner. I had heard about the butter burgers they serve there and I gotta try one.

4:15pm

We're sitting at the counter at Solly's, which really just reminds me of a diner from back home. When you order a butter burger, you're literally ordering a heart attack on a bun. No joke. There's not one, not two, not three, but four (*four!*) burger patties, a pile of hot, stewed onions, and on top of that, about half a stick of butter dripping down the sides of the burger tower. Krystal thought this was cheese but quickly realized it wasn't. (Cheese, by the way, is optional).

I have to say that it is absolutely delicious but about three quarters of the way through, my heart started skipping, I started sweating, and I had to sit back, take a little break and some deep breaths before finishing it off. (It probably wasn't the best idea to finish...) They need to think about building a hospital next door... or, at the very least, issuing a defibrillator with every order.

In Miller Park right now and although I'm in a coma from the butter burger, I'm eating the famous brat with the Stadium Secret Sauce, similar to the mustard in Cleveland. I think it tastes good but I gotta tell ya – that butter burger seriously made me a bit delusional and I think I'm passing in and out of consciousness.

Miller Park is absolutely huge and from its giant domed shape and flying buttress-like arms that support its retractable roof, it looked like an alien mothership when I first saw it from the highway. But it's nice inside, with the twisty slide out in the outfield and the famous Sausage Race that pits Brat, Italian Sausage, Polish Sausage, Hot Dog and Chorizo against each other in a race around the field. Hot Dog won tonight.

10:48pm

Joey is driving to the Water Street Brewery and I am in the passenger seat with a terrible stomachache. My body is screaming for mercy and I hear it but there's one more thing I have to eat tonight – the Scotch Eggs.

The Scotch Eggs... an almost divine creation that seems too good to be true. It's a hard-boiled egg, wrapped in sausage, then deep-fried and served with a dipping sauce.

We made it to the bar just in time to order some before the kitchen closed. I made it only about halfway through the egg until I surrendered. I couldn't do it. I literally could not take another bite. My body was finally rejecting it and I was beginning to crave something nutritious.

"Do you have like a bowl of lettuce or a piece of fruit or something… or a carrot would be great," I asked the bartender.

She looked confused. "You want like a salad?"

"No, I just want a banana or something. Just a raw veggie or fruit."

She came back with a whole tomato, which I ate like an apple in my hand. I never tasted anything more delicious than that tomato. I could literally feel the nutrients running through my bloodstream and my digestive tract rejoicing that there's finally something healthy to work with.

By the end of the night in Milwaukee, our poor diets had peaked to Ruthian proportions. Along the way, we had completely reconstructed the food pyramid, substituting meats with hotdogs and jerky, vegetables with cheese fries, grains with beer, fruits with watermelon Bubblicious and whatever other shit we were putting into our bodies. That tomato was the first piece of real vegetable I've had since we left... about 2 weeks ago??

Although I had a nice bed and as tired as I was, I felt sick and I did not sleep well tonight. If I want to live to see the age of 26, I'm going to have to make some changes to my diet sooner, rather than later.

Friday, May 1 — DAY 14
Chicago, Part 2 — Northside
1:05 Game @ Wrigley Field (Ballpark #17)
Total Miles Today — 93
Total Miles So Far — 5,067

8:00am

"Nice morning," Joey said from the passenger seat as he bit into his first apple in 14 days. He didn't sleep well last night, either, but that was more because he was concerned about the ghost of Jeffrey Dahmer getting him.

"Something kept tugging at my toes last night," he told me. "And I couldn't sleep because I kept feeling it but there wasn't anything there. It was Dahmer, though. I know it. Dahmer was trying to eat my toes."

"Dahmer didn't die there so it wouldn't have been *his* ghost," I reasoned. "If it was a ghost, it probably was one of his victims and they weren't violent people so they probably weren't trying to hurt you."

I had one beer last night but I feel hungover as hell today so it must be from the food. I'm starting off on a different track this morning – I'm having oatmeal with fresh fruits instead of a sausage and egg McMuffin from McDonalds. So delicious... and I don't even like oatmeal.

10:00am

At Chicago O'Hare dropping off Krystal. Pedro got out to walk her to the door.

"Is Pedro crying?" Joey asks. "I think Pedro's crying."

Pedro got back in the Vanbino and I looked at him through the rear-view mirror. He was gazing out his window as we made our way to Chicago's north side. I could see that his eyes were sad.

"Only a couple more weeks till you can see her again," I said.

"I know, not bad. I've never been away from her for this long... I love her. I love Krystal."

11:15am

Wrigleyville is booming! Man, what a scene! "The Friendly Confines" (as dubbed by Mr. Cub himself) sits smack in the middle of the neighborhood it inspired. Similar to Fenway, it fills a city block and is surrounded by bars and pubs, restaurants and homes… yes, homes. And on top of some of these bars and homes are bleachers on the roof so fans can literally watch the games from across the street. There's the Cubby Bear… and Murphy's… and everywhere little reminders of the current drought the Cubbie loyal are suffering through. One sign declares 'It's Gonna Happen!' and another pleads 'Break the Curse!' The last time the Cubs won a World Series was in 1908 – Teddy Roosevelt was in office, the Model T was introduced, and a loaf of bread cost five cents. In fact, the last time the Cubs even *appeared* in a World Series was when World War II was just ending.

On Waveland Avenue, which borders Wrigley along the outfield, there is an opening in the ballpark's stucco façade and instead of a wall there is a gate. It's a doorway for loading and unloading, I guess, but you can see straight through and out onto the field from the sidewalk. Some people stand around, a father with his young son on his shoulders, a family, look through the gate to watch batting practice. So old-fashioned and so great the Cubs allow anybody to watch from the street.

Here's something I found interesting – Wrigley Field was built in 1916 for $250,000, or $5.46 million in today's money, and it was built in just six weeks. The new Yankee Stadium, on the other hand, was built for $1.5 billion ($1.54 billion in today's money) and it took just under three years to complete. After taking everything that Wrigley has to offer – the hand-turned scoreboard, the famous red marquee at the entrance, the brick outfield walls coated thick with ivy, the Old Styles and the hotdogs and the "Take Me Out" renditions, that little opening on Waveland and the entire neighborhood itself – this has everything that Yankee Stadium needs, and it proves that money can't buy charm.

Wrigleyville reminded me a lot of the Fenway neighborhood in Boston and, like in Boston, it's hard not to be a fan of the home team. The fans are so passionate, are smart, and are so in-tune with their team that it is more than just a game for them – it's their way of life. From April through September (hopefully through October soon for these fans) entire days and weekends are planned around when the Cubs are playing. They talk about players on their team like they are friends. And, while observing these fans over a beer in the Cubby Bear, I realized just how loyal this fan-base really is and how amazing it is for the entire Cub Nation to keep on rallying behind a team year in and year out that hasn't won in a century. It's inspiring.

Our seats are in the top row, third base side. There's a fence to our backs and the wind is blowing in directly on us. It's May 1 but it feels like it's January – here I am in my winter jacket, my scarf and snow hat, sitting in a baseball game and still FREEZING! I mean, literally *freezing*! (As cold as I am, I still have an Old Style. I can't come to Wrigley and not get an Old Style... c'mon!) Now I know why they call it the Windy City. I CANNOT wait till we get down south in a couple days. I checked the forecast for Tampa and it's 85 and sunny. What I would give for 85 and sunny right now... Still, regardless of the cold, at least it's not raining... and at least our quest is still alive after the doom-and-gloom forecast from the first two weeks.

4:30pm

The Cubbies beat the Fish 8-6 today and as we made our way out onto Sheffield, the team raised their white 'W' flag above the scoreboard (a tradition that started in 1937) and the neighborhood was filled with the melody of 'Go Cubs Go,' a song they play here after every Cubs win.

"How you feeling today?" Pedro asked me.

"Much better." Krystal also made me eat some granola and OJ for breakfast this morning and I had a salad at the Cubby Bear before the game for lunch. Already I'm feeling healthier.

5:50pm

The Billy Goat Tavern.

The name alone can strike fear in any Cubs fan heart and send a chill down their spine. It sits under Michigan Avenue, small and unassuming in the shadows of the alley-like streetscape, and is almost invisible to the average pedestrian. But it is there, lurking in the background, preying on the dreams of the innocent Cubs fan.

And it is here, where in 1945 (the last time the Cubs appeared in the World Series) the curse was entrenched on the team and is widely regarded as the reason they haven't been back since. (It is also the last curse remaining in the Majors after the Red Sox broke their "Curse of the Bambino" with a World Series title in '04).

So what exactly happened in 1945? We sat down with the manager and over some cheeseburgers and beers, he told us the story:

It happened on October 6, Game 4 of the 1945 World Series against the Tigers with the series tied at two games. William "Billy" Sianis, owner of the Billy Goat Tavern, had two box seat tickets to the game – one for himself and one for his pet goat, which he brought hoping to bring his Cubbies some luck. Upon entering the gates

135

however, he was ejected on the grounds "no animals allowed in the ballpark."

Billy angrily appealed to the Cubs owner P. K. Wrigley who said, "you can stay, but the goat has to go."

"Why no goat?" Billy asked.

"Because the goat stinks." The remark enraged Billy and he proclaimed, "the Cubs ain't gonna win no more. The Cubs ain't never gonna win a World Series so long as the goat is not allowed in Wrigley Field."

The Cubs went on to lose Game 4 and were swept the rest of the series. After losing, Billy sent a telegram to P. K. Wrigley that simply asked, "Who stinks now?"

Since that fateful autumn day in October, the Cubs, from 1945-2009 have compiled only 15 winning seasons, finished in first place only 3 times, won 0 pennants, appeared in the postseason just 4 times, and not once have they made a World Series appearance. Now if that's not a curse, I don't know what is.

I asked the manager (a Cubs fan) if he thinks the curse will ever be lifted. "I don't know," he replied in a soft, almost somber voice. "I would love to see it be lifted but that's up to the Billy Goat." Then he smiled a helpless smile and shrugged his shoulders.

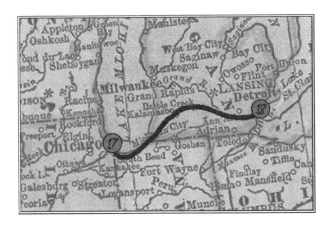

Saturday, May 2 — DAY 15
Detroit
1:05 Game @ Comerica Park (Ballpark #18)
Total Miles Today — 283
Total Miles So Far — 5,350

The three of us were too tired to drive last night so we parked in a rest stop right around Battle Creek, Michigan about two hours due west from Detroit. It's cold outside but it's supposed to warm up by game time. For the first day in over a week, there was no rain in the forecast.

12:15pm

Andy and a group of his friends are tailgating and they welcomed us nomads in for some food and some beer. "You guys should check out the old Tiger Stadium before you leave," Andy suggests as he points in its direction.

137

"It's still standing?" I asked. "I thought they tore it down after Comerica opened."

Andy smiles, "Well, half of it is, at least. It probably won't be for much longer so you should check it out while you can."

4:15pm

The game today at Comerica was a good one. The Tigers scored 5 in the 4th but that didn't last long because in the top of the 5th, the Indians came right back and matched them. The Indians ended up taking a 7-6 lead but the Tigers rallied in the 8th to score 3 and ended up winning 9-7.

4:45pm

I'm standing at the intersection of Michigan and Trumbull, a spot so famous that it's known simply as "The Corner." Before me stands the sad remains of Tiger Stadium, a once proud ballpark. All that stands now is the grandstand behind home plate and a flagpole out in center. As I look through the 10-foot high chain-link fence I see the gift shop and the ticket windows, now all boarded up. I look up and see the logo of the big 'D' with the Tiger pouncing through its center, its colors now faded by the sun.

I walk down the first base side and the vast expanse of the field opens before me. I look out and think about all the things this site has witnessed in its 104 years of hosting professional baseball – the greatness of Cobb, the power of Ruth, the glory of four World Championships...

Yes, this is the Corner where the Babe not only hit #700 but also hit the longest homerun in the history of the game – a mammoth moon shot that soared close to 600 feet…

This is the Corner, where an ailing Lou Gehrig removed himself from the lineup after starting 2,130 consecutive games…

This is the Corner that Ty Cobb called home for 21 seasons, collected over 4,000 hits and earned a .367 career batting average (the highest ever) in the era of the pitcher…

The glory that has happened on this patch of earth can easily be overlooked, for now it is overgrown with tall grass and weeds. The faint outline of the infield, of the base paths, of home plate can now just barely be made out and a puny little hill, once the pitchers mound, has succumbed to the wild weeds. Tiger Stadium was once the jewel of this blue-collar town but today it looks forgotten.

I see a man with a little girl standing along the fence where the outfield once was and he is pointing out towards the grandstand and tells her something. It looks like he has some stories to share so I went up and introduced myself.

Jeff and his daughter Liddy were at the Tigers game today but afterwards he wanted to show her where he grew up.

"This is a part of my childhood man, Tiger Stadium. I love Comerica but, man, nothing can replace the memories from here and my daughter has to know where I came from… where her dad came from… because I don't know how much longer this is gonna be standing." Liddy, I'd say about six years old or so, in a Tigers hat and pigtails, looks up at me from under her dad's arm and shows me a Tiger finger puppet that she holds on her pinky.

"I remember the one game I was here, all my friends got so mad at me cause I was talking and Cecil Fielder hit the home run that went over the stadium! And we all missed it cause I was talkin'!" Jeff cracks up as he looks out towards right field then stops laughing but his gaze continues. "Lotta memories here... lotta memories. And it's a shame cause it's all gone now..." he turns to me, "but that's the way it is. That's the way it is."

Jeff and Liddy wished us luck on our quest before taking off. As I watched them walk off, I realized that as forgotten as this old park appears, it is not forgotten at all – memories from fans like Jeff keep it alive. I wanted to get inside those fences so bad and get out onto that field with my camera. I wanted to film what is left because, for all I know, this might be the last chance for anyone. There was a security guard, though, pacing the premises like a tiger in a cage and he would no doubt see us if we tried to sneak in.

"Let's grease him," Joey suggested. "You ever done that before?"

"No," I said. Pedro was laughing. "You?"

"No," Joey replied. He had that glisten in his eye that he gets when he's up to something. That glisten, I've come to learn, usually means trouble. "How much cash you got?

I look in my pockets. "Three bucks."

"75 cents." Pedro hands over three quarters.

"I only got a five…" Joey shakes his head, "not enough."

Lucky for us, there was a gas station across the street and where there's a gas station, there's an ATM.

I walked back over to the Corner with a wad of five 20's gripped in my fist, feeling shady and slick, cool and confident like I was James Cagney in one of his classic Hollywood roles.

A little trailer sat way out in left field, about 40 yards inside the fence and we went up and hung around there. Last time I saw the security guard, he was walking around the grandstand but I think he had since retired into the quarters.

Thirty minutes pass with no sign of him. "Where the hell did this guy go??"

"He's watching us… waiting for us to slip in," Joey said.

Another twenty minutes. How long do we wait? I was growing impatient.

"Trav, just let me go in," Pedro said. He had been silent this whole time and I now knew why – he had been working on a plan. "I'll jump that outside gate (points towards center field) then Joey can slide the camera underneath and I'll run in and get some shots. As soon as I see the guy I'll come running back. What's the worst that can happen?"

I was sick of waiting. "Let's do it."

We didn't know the capacity of the security force (we weren't anticipating it being much but we had to be careful because I don't want the reason for us failing the Trip being us going to jail for trespassing) so we took our time and formulated a getaway plan. This is how it would go down – since Pedro is the skinniest and, most importantly, the fastest of us, he would be the one to enter. Joey would stand just outside the center field fence. He had two jobs – to slip Pedro the camera once he was inside and, most importantly, to signal to me when he saw Pedro running back. I would be waiting in the parking lot of Briggs Lumber across the street sitting idle in the Vanbino. I'd keep an eye on Joey waiting for the signal and, once I got it, I'll peel out, pick them up, and speed off into the cool night.

Flawless.

I backed the Vanbino into the parking lot (the back sliding door wide open) and watched Pedro slip under the outfield fence. It was just high enough from the ground for him to clear it. Joey slipped the camera under and it disappeared. I could not see Pedro at this point, only Joey, and so I kept a keen eye on him, waiting for the signal.

One minute passed… two… three… seems like twenty minutes. I'm watching Joey and Joey's watching Pedro.

Another minute… then another. The sun is getting lower in the sky behind the grandstand.

Then Joey's arm flies into the air waving violently in a panic. The signal! Holy shit the signal!!

I throw the Vanbino into gear and peel out leaving a cloud of smoke and some burned rubber behind.

I see the camera emerge from under the fence followed quickly by Pedro and the two of them run in a frenzy towards the van. I can see through the mesh fence a shadow of a figure running across the field in our direction. Joey and Pedro get to the curb the second I arrive and I slow down but I don't stop. They jump into the open side door and with legs and arms flailing inside and outside the van, I speed off.

Holy shit that was awesome! Adrenaline was pumping and I think I finally breathed for the first time in ten minutes. Then I began laughing. "Did you get the shots?!"

"Aww, dude, I got 'em!" Pedro said with a huge smile. "But I wanna go back. I wanna get the sunset."

"Go back? Dude, they're probably keeping an eye out for our van," I said.

"We'll be fine, we'll be fine. We'll stake out across the street. And it's getting dark out, too. They'll never see us."

So I drove around the block and crept slowly back through the Briggs lot and finally parked in the shadows between two buildings. Pedro mounted the camera on his tripod and started to record.

We hung out on the hood and the roof of the Vanbino eating some peanut butter and jelly sandwiches watching the spectacular sunset show before us from our front row seats. The sun sank lower and lower into the Michigan sky, turning the grandstand into a silhouette against a canvas of bright pinks, oranges, and yellows. It was breathtaking, it really was.

"Comerica was nice," Joey said. "I thought it was too "Disneyland" at first with the tiger statues all around but in the end I really liked it."

"It was neat that they have like a little carnival, too, you know?" Pedro said. Pedro was talking about the amusement area for kids that has a little Ferris wheel and carousel.

"I thought the statues out in center were cool," I said.

The sun eventually disappeared behind the remains of Tiger Stadium and we were left in the dark. For a while, no one said anything... we just sat with our thoughts. I was thinking of Jeff talking about his Tiger Stadium and Tom from St. Louis talking about his old Busch and how profoundly their ballparks had impacted their lives... how their ballpark wasn't just a place where they visited, but it was a place where they grew up. Then I started thinking about our Trip – halfway done but so much still ahead.

"Atlanta?" Joey asked.

"Atlanta," I confirmed.

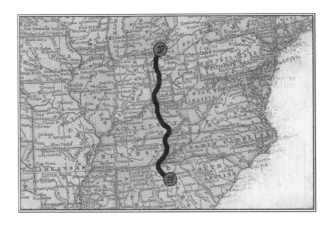

Sunday, May 3 — DAY 16
Atlanta
1:05 Game @ Turner Field (Ballpark #19)
Total Miles Today — 723
Total Miles So Far — 6,073

1:10am

Right now we're on I-75 somewhere in between
Dayton and Cincinnati. My shift is over and now Pedro's
going to take the wheel. We still have a good nine hours
until we hit Atlanta and we have a 1:00 game today so
tonight would have to be pretty much all driving. Joey's in
the back getting some sleep now and I'm going to try and do
the same.

7:22am

Overnight, we continued on I-75 and passed through Lexington and Knoxville, and now we're just passing through Chattanooga. Just a little over two hours left till Atlanta.

9:45am

We found a Waffle House (it's actually not hard – like Dunkin' Donuts in Boston, there's literally one on every corner down here) so we stopped for some breakfast. I'm starving and I'm desperate for a cup of hot coffee.

11:00am

We're in the parking lot of Turner Field and we noticed that the Braves made a similar move as the White Sox with preserving their ballpark predecessor. Like Comiskey, the footprint of Fulton County Stadium is outlined in the Turner Field parking lot, complete with a plaque where the old home plate once sat, foul lines, and a pitching rubber. And in the outfield, 330 feet away from home plate across the brick and asphalt is a section of fence with the number 715 on it.

We're tailgating with some new friends we made before the game who have their little chihuahua here with them, dressed in a Braves jersey and all ready for the game. Today is "Bring Your Dog to the Ballpark Day" so if you bring your dog today, you're allowed to bring it into the ballpark with you. There are dogs everywhere. This tailgate family is great – it's a mom and a dad (older and both retired) tailgating the game with their two grown kids and

146

their families. The spread they have is amazing – there's a couple linen-covered card tables with grilled burgers, dogs and brats, home-made casseroles and veggie dishes, chips, pretzels, pickles, pies and cakes. It's gourmet... it's a gourmet tailgate. Sherry, the mom, and I bonded and when I told her about our diets, she gasped in horror and lost her breath for a moment. With a hand over her heart, she said – "well, my-my, we're going to have to change that." Sherry proceeded to pack us up some doggie bags of their food for us to take on the road.

"I hope your mother doesn't know what you've been eating," she said as she filled two big Tupperware containers of all their fixins for us. I went to college in Georgia and lived here five years and this is the kind of southern hospitality I remember.

"Thank you," I say to her. "This means a lot to us." She gave us hugs and told us to be careful.

2:15pm

I was basking in the sun inside Turner – after a couple weeks of sitting through cold baseball, we were finally where it was warm and sunny. It felt great. I couldn't believe it was just two days ago that we were freezing in Wrigley. I looked over at Pedro – he was reclined in his seat soaking up the rays. He loves this heat.

5:15pm

Before embarking on the eight and a half hour road trip to Tampa Bay, we stopped for some dinner at a little bar and grill we found on the way out of Atlanta called

Stillwater, home of a famous drink called "The Hurricane."
It was packed and the only tables were outside, so that's
where we sat. We were surprised that there was outdoor
seating because those are usually the tables that go first but
there was a whole bunch. Weird... it's a beautiful evening.

Just as we got our food the rain poured down on us.
Luckily, there was an umbrella over our table but that only
did so much in this heavy rain. Our backs got soaked but no
big deal – at least my hushpuppies stayed dry. Now I know
why all the outside tables were empty – we were the only
ones who didn't know the forecast.

Monday, May 4 — DAY 17
Tampa Bay
7:35 Game @ Tropicana Field (Ballpark #20)
Total Miles Today — 479
Total Miles So Far — 6,552

9:00am

Aaaaahhhhhhhhh….. Florida! Wonderful, beautiful, sunny, warm Florida! The first two weeks of cold temps and storm-dodging are now just memories and the blue skies and warm air that surround me now seems like a dream. And it could not have come at a better time.

Today is just past the midway point of the Trip and in our first 15 days, we've already been to 20 parks and driven close to 7,000 miles. The dual responsibilities of driving and filming have worn us down and we're going to treat our time in Tampa like a mini-vacation to recharge our batteries and get us set for the really long drives that still loom ahead.

Lucky for us, Jackie and Jill (the sisters we stayed with in Queens) and their parents own a condo ten minutes from Tropicana. So when they offered us the keys for the night, we gladly accepted.

12:30pm

It doesn't get any better than this.

"Bronzing poolside," as Joey says. "Gotta do it for the babes." The pool sits on the bay and Joey, Pedro and I lounge with our blender full of pina colada, relaxing, unwinding, taking it all in.

Aside from the one other girl sunbathing in a lounge chair on the other side of the pool, we have it to ourselves. Joey swears that it's Lindsay Lohan over there and I have to admit that it does look like her. But she's wearing those stupid fly-eye sunglasses that cover three quarters of her face so it's hard to tell.

The Rays play at seven tonight but for now I don't want to think about baseball or the Trip. I just want to relax by the pool with my pina colada.

1:15pm

So Joey might have been right… that girl on the other side of the pool just left but on her way out she passed by us and commented on our camera. She had auburn hair, freckles, and a raspy voice… just like Lindsay.

150

Joey and I just kind of looked at each other after she left. We were both thinking the same thing.

"Dude... holy shit," he said in shock. "Why didn't I offer her a pina colada?? That's the whole reason I made the pina colada, for the babes. I was frozen, though. I was scared... like a frightened little puppy. I couldn't move." A long pause. "Dude, it was her. That was Lindsay."

"Maybe," I said.

"That wasn't Lindsay," Pedro said.

5:15pm

Is it bad if I admit that I don't want to go to the game tonight? Sitting on the balcony in my shorts with a Heineken, watching the boaters and the pelicans drift by, the warm breeze rustling the palms... this is paradise. A blue heron stands still in the shallows, hunting for fish. He's been there for about 45 minutes now and has had a couple unsuccessful attempts at catching his dinner so far.

Joey walks out and joins me on the balcony with a beer.

"How about we cancel the rest of the Trip and just hang here for the next two weeks? I'd be down for that," I say to him.

"I gotta think some things through, dude," he starts. "I mean seriously, what am I doing living above a cheesesteak place in South Philly? I mean seriously... especially when there's all this out here. The sun, the heat, the beaches, the pools, the beautiful babes, the pina coladas… and here I am living in a shack in cold, crummy South Philly." He pauses as he looks out at the view. "Oh, I gotta think some things through here. When I get back I'm gonna have to make some changes."

Since we're treating this stay in Florida like a mini-vacation, we decided to go to a real restaurant and get some real food. I am trying to eat better since my physical breakdown in Milwaukee and I've been pretty good but it's so hard staying on a healthy diet when you're moving around as much as we are.

I talked to Jackie earlier today and she told us about St. Pete Pier, so we headed down that way and found this great little restaurant on the water. We ate out on the deck along the harbor and I had some of the best pork chops I've ever had. They came on a bed of roasted cherries… that's right, cherries. Believe it. Skeptical? So was I. But don't be – it's delicious.

Tropicana Field was only so-so. I wasn't expecting much to begin with, though, so I wasn't disappointed. We did have some great seats on the lower level right behind home plate, so that was good. And the stingray tank in the outfield is something neat to see, as well, but other than that, there's not a whole lot going on here. They're trying to get a new park, I think, so hopefully they can. Florida is just too nice to play baseball inside. The visiting O's trumped their hosts tonight 8-4 on the strength of a Markakis 3-run shot.

Back at the condo, Joey sits out on the balcony in his bare feet with a Corona keeping watch for another Lindsay sighting. Pedro and I threw a load of laundry in for the first time this trip – it'll be nice to finally wear clean clothes. Really looking forward to it. Pedro and I mixed our clothes to save time and when we asked Joey if he wanted to throw anything in, he asked – "you guys are mixing??"

"Yeah," I answer. "We wanna get to bed soon."

"I'll throw a load in when yours is done," he replied. "I don't really wanna mix batches. It's weird. All our underwear swirling around together..." he looks disgusted. "I don't think so."

"What's the difference?" Pedro asks. "It's in hot water and soap."

"I'll throw a load in when yours is done."

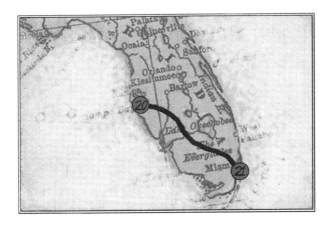

Tuesday, May 5 — DAY 18
Miami
7:05 Game @ Dolphin Stadium (Ballpark #21)
Total Miles Today — 282
Total Miles So Far — 6,834
Happy Cinco de Mayo!

11:30am

Well, our little vacay was nice while it lasted but now it's back to business. We have twelve days and only ten parks left but now the driving gets serious and we'll be using entire days just for those long drives.

Today is Cinco de Mayo and where better to celebrate Mexican heritage than in Miami? We're leaving the condo in Tampa now, going to stop for some fresh-squeezed OJ (need my Vitamin C) and drive the 280 miles south. We should get to Landshark Stadium (or is it still called Dolphin Stadium? I can't keep up) by 4:30, 5:00 at the latest.

Joey's cousin TJ lives in Miami and he met us in the parking lot for a little tailgating. Dolphin Stadium, by far, has the best set-up for tailgating. Each strip of asphalt is divided by a large strip of grass so people park on the pavement and back-up to the grass to tailgate. It's really great but unfortunately is underused during baseball games.

TJ showed up with a case of Peroni in his trunk and we tailgated with him. It's a shame how little people this park attracts. The Marlins have the misfortune of playing in a stadium that was built for football but it is also about 40 miles from Miami, and some Marlins fans we were talking to say that is a reason for their low attendance. We ended up hanging out with these guys for a while and, conveniently enough, they had four extra tickets and they gave them to us. The seats were 20 rows behind first base side.

These fans giving us these tickets really made me realize something – the one thing that stands out above all else on this Trip so far is the fans, in every city, at every park. How welcoming everyone is, opening their tailgates to us, treating us like old friends. Everyone has been so genuinely giving without expecting or wanting anything in return. So far, we haven't had one bad experience.

10:30pm

The Fish were shutout by Volquez and the Reds 7-0 tonight and after the game, TJ took us down to South Beach.

"You're in Miami on Cinco de Mayo?? Rock on," TJ said in his mellow, chill, rock star-like tone. "When's your next game?"

"Two days in Houston," Joey told him.

TJ nodded. "So we got plenty of time then. You guys seriously might not make it out alive. It's cool, though. I'll make sure you get to Houston on time."

11:35pm

Ocean Drive, South Beach... a different world. And of any night to experience South Beach in all its glory, it is tonight. On one side of the street are the bars, the restaurants and the hotels in art deco style buildings and on the other side is a palm-lined park, then the dunes, then the ocean.

We weave in and out of the throngs of people and street-side tables as TJ leads us to his favorite place in South Beach. The girls here are almost as dressed up (or as dressed down, depending on how you look at it) as the Rolls Royces and the Mercedes that cruise down the street with their pounding music. After walking a few blocks, to see a girl in nothing but stilettos, a thong, and fishnet stockings is not unusual... that seems to be the norm, in fact. And that's not even making a fashion statement; the real statement comes from the ones wearing the live snakes around their necks.

We get to the spot and sit down at an outside table. The weather (who am I kidding – the people watching) is too good to stay indoors. A nice, cool breeze blows off the ocean and across the street.

The waiter arrives. "Four mojitos," TJ orders. Then he looks at us. "They're the best. Trust me."

"You kinda look like Donny Wahlberg," Pedro tells TJ.

"I get that all the time. I get Mark sometimes, too, but mostly Donny. Check this out…" TJ pulls a couple of folded pictures from his wallet and hands them to Joey. Joey unfolds them and his mouth drops open when he realizes what they are.

"Oh, wow… oh my god…" he says in disbelief. He passes them to Pedro and I. "That's my car, after the accident I was telling you about." The story that Joey had told at Niagara was no exaggeration – his car was literally a crumpled ball of metal stuck in the branches of a tree. He really must have a guardian angel watching out for him.

"My mom sent me those pictures," TJ said. "She told me to always keep them on you so they remind you to never speed." Joey takes the pictures back and studies them closer.

He shakes his head in disbelief. "Unbelievable, dude."

The mojitos arrived and I immediately realized why TJ liked these so much. As the waiter placed one down in front of me I had to tilt my head up to see the top. The stalk of sugar cane rose a good foot above the rim of the glass and the minty rum tasted sweet and refreshing as I sipped it.

"You could beat a man with that," Pedro said.

I looked up at TJ and he was looking back at me with a little smirk on his face. "Told ya to trust me," he said.

After dinner, we hung out on the beach for a bit under an almost-full moon. By 1:00, we decided it was about time to hit the road. It's a 20-hour drive to Houston but our game isn't for two days so our idea is to drive the 14 hours to New Orleans and spend tomorrow night on Bourbon Street.

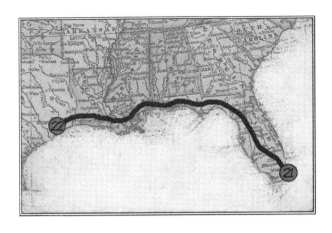

Wednesday & Thursday, May 6 & 7 — DAYS 19 & 20
Driving Day then Houston
7:35 Game @ Minute Maid Park (Ballpark #22)
Total Miles Today — 1,186
Total Miles So Far — 8,020

5:12 am

We're somewhere on Florida's Turnpike which seemingly NEVER ENDS! I feel like I've been driving forever and not getting anywhere. We've also spent $24 in tolls on this freaking road… I hate it.

I'm stopped on the side of the road right now because Joey is throwing up again. I'm standing outside, too, to stretch my legs and as the flashing taillights splash Joey in bright, red light, he throws up some more.

He looks up at me, hands on knees, his eyes watering and red and begging for mercy.

"You alright, man?" I say chuckling.

"I knew I shouldn't have gotten that pesto. That weasel of a waiter talked me into it though..." he manages to speak. "Every time I think I'm gonna like the pesto but it never works out that way...." He spits. "Or it was those coffee creamers from the gas station. They weren't on ice. I never trust those things. It's milk! Why isn't it on ice?!" He takes a deep breath and exhales then spits. Then he chugs a whole bottle of water without once coming up for air.

"You good?" I ask.

"Yeah, I'm good." We walk to the Vanbino then he stops and turns around. "Wait, let me just take a leak."

1:00pm

A little past Gainesville, we veered west and followed the panhandle through Tallahassee and Pensacola, then passed through Mobile, Alabama and Biloxi, Mississippi until finally arriving in Louisiana. By now, the tree and grass-lined highway had turned into swampy bayous and I knew NOLA had to be close.

Thank God we're out of Florida. I never realized how big of a state it is – it honestly felt like it was never-ending. That drive sucked.

3:30pm

Finally rolled into downtown New Orleans and got a room at the Holiday Inn in the French Quarter.

162

Up in the room, Pedro thought it would be funny to hide in the closet and jump out after I came back from getting some ice. Joey thought it was funny, too.

I didn't. I nearly shit my pants.

"Dude, if you couldn't handle Miami last night, there's no way you're gonna survive New Orleans," I said to Joey.

"It was the coffee creamers, man. I only had that one mojito last night. Why weren't they on ice?? Milk has to be on ice!" Joey started getting angry again, then calmed down. "I feel great now, though. I feel like a million bucks."

I feel good, too. I didn't sleep at all last night and I'm not tired at all now. It's New Orleans, baby! I can't sleep! What did that hotel desk clerk say last week? She'll sleep when she's dead? Well, same here.

10:15am, the next day. . .

"This van is really starting to smell like shit," Joey says from the passenger seat. He's digging around in his bag for something.

"I know," Pedro agrees. "As soon as we have time we should clean it out."

Joey hands us both a One-A-Day. "Eat 'em up. You need your vitamins."

My head is pounding and I think I might still be a little drunk. Bourbon Street... Jesus, what a crazy place. I remember starting out with a few Hand Grenades at Tropical

Isle then getting some shots at the Olde Absinthe House. Then I remember listening to some Dixie music at a German bar. Then after that – nothing. That's the last thing I remember. But we watched back some of the tapes from yesterday and there was footage of us on stage with some dueling pianos at a stranger's wedding reception in O'Neill's. What a crazy night. I love this town.

And all I can say is thank God for the always-responsible Pedro because he was the one back at the hotel early last night, the one who woke us on time this morning, and the one who is sober to drive today. If we successfully finish this Trip, it will be because of him.

We're stopping at Café Du Monde for some much needed coffee and beignets then it's back onto I-10 for the six hour trip to Houston.

5:45pm

We swung around Baton Rouge and now watched the scenery transform from swamps and bayous to rocky hills and dry fields, until finally arriving in Houston. Our first stop in Houston wasn't Minute Maid Park, however – it was the Astros old home, the legendary Astrodome.

It's still standing but is in a state of disrepair (not nearly to the extent that Tiger Stadium is in, though). When it opened in 1965, it was the first dome and it was so large that it was dubbed the Eighth Wonder of the World. It now sits empty in the shadows of Reliant Stadium, and what really struck me as amazing is how this onetime giant is now dwarfed beside the Texan's home.

We entered Minute Maid Park through Union Station, the historic train depot from 1911 that was acquired, restored, and incorporated into the ballpark by the Astros and now serves as the main entrance to the ballpark. There's a free giveaway today but it's a strange one… it's not exactly the typical travel mug we got at Wrigley or the tee-shirt we got from the Orioles.

"Why a diamond?" Joey asks as he looks at the tiny diamond stud in the little plastic baggie.

"What is the diamond anniversary? 50th?" I ask.

Pedro shakes his head. "I think 60th."

This is not the 60th anniversary year for the Astros – the team was established in '62… and Minute Maid opened in 2000, so it's not that either.

So I asked one of the guys handing them out at the gate.

"You know, it's just a nice little thank you for you fans," was his answer with a smile. I could tell that he's been asked that a lot today and it sounded like his way of saying "Beat it, kid. Hell if I know."

"Bubba will know. Where we meeting him?" Joey asked as he stopped to take a picture of the train in the outfield.

"Out in left center. He said we can't miss him." Bubba is a Houston native. He grew up an Astros fan (hard not to with the likes of Biggio and Bagwell) and when he heard about our Trip, he emailed us.

"I started a little fan club a couple years ago for Berkman and now we've grown to over 30 members," Bubba wrote. "Howard has the Homers and all these other great hitters have their little group of fans at the yard and I felt the Big Puma needed one, too. So we're the Little Pumas. We come to every home game in puma costumes."

Bubba was right – we couldn't miss them. In fact, we could see the gathering of pumas from the opposite side of the park. When we arrived to the Puma Porch way out in left-center, Bubba was the first to greet us.

"Thanks for the tickets, man," I said shaking his hand. Bubba had generously left three tickets for us at will call.

"Absolutely, friend. Glad you guys made it!"

"Us, too." There are probably about 15 to 20 people here, all dressed in identical puma costumes from head to toe. "Where do you get the costumes?" I ask, impressed.

"I found some site online that sells them for pretty cheap. The quality isn't great but whatever, right? It's all about the presentation. And Lance loves it."

"Oh yeah?"

"Yeah. He invited us onto the field before a game last year so he could take a picture with us. Then he gave us all autographs."

"That's awesome," I tell him. Ironically, Berkman just struck out at the plate.

"What's the deal with the giveaway tonight?" I ask Bubba.

"Dude, I have no idea." He laughs. "I don't think anybody does."

Bubba unzips a little duffle bag and pulls out a puma costume. "So I have an extra puma suit tonight... who wants to be an honorary puma?"

Pedro and I both look at Joey. He is leaning up against the wall and after a moment of hesitation, gives in. "Alright! Suit me up!"

It was funnier than usual watching Joey tonight because he acted like himself... exactly like himself. He waited in line for beers, ate a foot-long chili cheese dog and a beef burrito, talked on the phone – but all while wearing a puma costume. I really think he forgot he had it on at times.

10:00pm

It's the bottom of the ninth right now and I literally *just missed* catching the ball from an Alfonso Soriano two-run shot in the top of the inning. And when I say 'just missed,' I mean *just missed* – the kid literally next to me caught it. That's the closest I've ever been to a homerun ball... well, any ball for that matter. I was at RFK a few years ago before the new Nats Park opened and I was in the upper deck, first base side. There was one other guy in my entire section sitting about 10 rows in front of me. A foul ball was hit up to us and landed about two rows behind that guy.

"Can I see that, man?" I asked him. I've always wanted to hold a game ball.

"No way," he said and walked off. I wasn't going to steal it. I just wanted to hold it for a second.

Berkman ended up going 0-5 with four strikeouts marking only the third time in his 10-year career that that's happened.

Sorry Big Puma. We're leaving now.

10:15pm

Cubs won 8-5 tonight after an exciting ninth that almost saw an Astros rally but they came up just a little short.

We know the drive that looms ahead of us now is a long one but we have a day and a half to reach LA so we're taking our time before pushing off.

There is a nice little park just outside Minute Maid beyond left field where we found a swinging bench to sit on. The roof to the ballpark is open for the first time tonight and I can see the homerun train sitting on top of the brick wall just behind me. This little park out here is nice – it's surrounded by gardens and the centerpiece is a baseball diamond with illuminated bases. Around the diamond are statues of Astros greats in action at their respective positions.

A little boy, probably four at the oldest, stands at the glowing home plate with a big, fat, plastic red bat. His dad softly lobs a white ball the size of a grapefruit towards him. The kid swings, connects – it's a slow dribbler back to the mound! He throws his bat and runs as hard as he can to first, his little Astros hat flying off. His dad fields it and runs to his son to tag him. He reaches him and the boy falls to the grass in a heap of laughter and the dad falls to the ground with him...

I remember playing ball with my dad. I remember him teaching me how to hit, how to throw, how to catch... I remember when he gave me his glove. His initials "S.G." were written in marker just beside the red Rawlings insignia and when he gave it to me, he added a "T." before the "S.G." to make it mine. Now *my* initials are on that glove. He showed me how to pound my fist in its deep pouch, how to oil it, how to take care of it. But the thing I remember most is the smell – that sweet, leathery smell of aged rawhide. To this day, whenever I smell that scent of leather, I think of that glove... of the day when my dad gave it to me and added my initial in front of his.

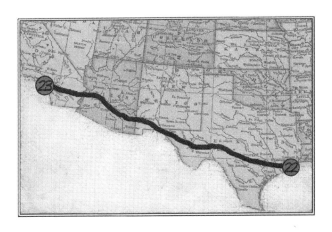

Friday & Saturday, May 8 & 9 — DAYS 21 & 22
Driving Day then Los Angeles
1:05 Game @ Dodger Stadium (Ballpark #23)
Total Miles Today — 1,549
Total Miles So Far — 9,569

8:30am

We decided to stop for the night in San Antonio, only three and half hours from Houston because we really want to see the Alamo. This may or may not have been a bad idea because now we have a shit-load of driving to do today and tonight.

"Excuse me, sir, is there anywhere around here to get some bagels?" I asked a sheriff patrolling the outside of the Alamo. We're on a dusty, little Texas street, low-key and mellow and hot in the blistering sun. I think it's true what they say because everything *is* bigger in Texas… and I have never, ever seen the sun as big in the sky as it is now.

The sheriff, with his bushy mustache, his cowboy hat and alligator boots, is tall and slender, and he looks down at me with a quizzical look. His thumbs are stuck inside his leather belt adorned with an enormous gold buckle with a horse on it.

"A who now?" he simply asks.

"Bagels?" I can see it's not processing so I continue, this time in more detail. "You know, bagels? They look like donuts but they're more like bread... you can put an egg on it..." My description is met with a befuddled look.

"Son, I'm afraid I don't know what you're saying to me. You can get some donuts over there." He points to a little place across the street.

"Okay, thank you." Holy shit.

10:15am

The site where Davey Crockett fell was extremely interesting and neat to see but we couldn't dilly-dally – 1,600 miles of road lay between us and Dodger Stadium and we only have 26 hours to cover it.

We did stop in the gift shop, though, and I guess since the last time Pedro scared me at the hotel in New Orleans was so successful and hilarious, he decided to do it again.

This time, he exploited my fear of snakes. Having found a toy snake in the gift shop, he tapped my shoulder and as I turned around, there was a snake in my face. It looked and moved like it was real and I thought it was until he keeled over in laughter.

I guess I screamed or jumped or something because a lot of people were looking at me. It took me a moment to catch my breath. "Dude, seriously… you'd better watch your back. You're two in the hole now."

I walked outside and saddled up in the Vanbino.

2:20pm

The speed limit on I-10 through Texas is 75 but Joey was going 90 when Officer Johnson pulled him over.

"Shit," Joey said as we watched the tall, slender officer exit his patrol car and walk up to the driver's side window. He poked his head inside the open window and gave each one of us a good, hard stare over the top rims of his Aviator sunglasses. Just like Officer "Bagel" in San Antonio, he, too, wore a cowboy hat, a giant belt buckle and some nice leather boots. Do they all dress like this down here?

"Son, I'm gonna need ya to step outta the car for me," he said to Joey, his thumbs tucked into his belt. 'Step out of the car?' I could tell we all thought that was strange. What happened to just asking for license and registration? Pedro didn't have to step out of the car when he was pulled over in Oklahoma.

Joey obliged. "Why don't you come back to my car with me cause you and I are gonna have a little talk."

What the hell?? Joey looked freaked out but he had no choice. Pedro and I exchanged befuddled looks.

"What's happening?" I asked Pedro.

"I don't know… this doesn't seem right…" he said.

We were both turned in our seats watching the scene unfold beside the patrol car about 90 feet behind us. Officer Johnson was about six inches taller than Joey and I could tell by his body language and the finger in Joey's face that he was yelling at him. Joey just kept nodding; he looked terrified, like a little preschooler getting reprimanded by his teacher. Then Officer Johnson folded his arms and leaned against his car as Joey started talking. He talked for a while and Officer Johnson listened. Five, maybe ten minutes passed before they both walked back to the Vanbino. They walked side-by-side, Officer Johnson laughing and them now looking like old friends.

Joey got back in and Officer Johnson leaned his head in through the window.

"You boys be safe now. There's some strong drifts comin' off these hills here and they'll blow ya right off the road. I've seen it before. Good luck now." He tipped his hat and walked off.

"What happened??" Pedro asked.

"He scolded me at first but he's a good man," Joey said. "He was just looking out for us."

"He give you a ticket?"

"Nah. Just a warning." Joey has the unique ability to charm anyone – man or woman, young or old – and he certainly charmed Officer Johnson.

Pedro was pissed that he got a $200 ticket but Joey got off with just a warning. "You son of a bitch," he said.

8:30pm

And I thought the drive through Florida was bad! I-10 through Texas is worse – the road is straight as an arrow and disappears into the horizon directly in front of you and into the horizon directly behind you. This drive is like a broken record. Standing in the middle of the road, you turn in a circle and every direction is identical. It's almost maddening. You drive 100, 200, 300 miles and it looks like you haven't moved an inch. I look out the right-side windows – nothing but flat, dry prairies for as far as the eye can see. I look out the left-side – the same. Are they prairies…? What is a prairie exactly? Is a prairie the same thing as a field? I think these are too dry for fields… there's tall grass but it's spotty and in clumps so I don't think it's desert quite yet. Is there grass in the desert? I see some oil drills dotting this barren landscape.

Anyway, we're pulled off to the side of the road right now to take a leak and watch the sunset. It's beautiful and somehow very different than the sunset in Detroit. The sky is a bright, glowing orange with some deep reds, cloudless, as the sun dips down below a low, rocky peak way off in the distance.

I think I just saw a roadrunner dart past.

Joey looks at me for a long moment. I can see that he is thinking and looks a bit confused almost. "Those things are real?"

"Roadrunners?" I ask

"Yeah. I thought it was just a cartoon."

"No, dude, they're real. Coyotes are real..."

"I know coyotes are real," he interjects.

"Yeah, roadrunners are real."

"Meep, meep," Pedro contributes.

We just entered New Mexico but before leaving Texas we drove through El Paso, which is literally on the U.S-Mexican border and we could see the town of Juarez on the other side with a Mexican flag the size of Delaware waving in the sky.

We still have about 13 hours of driving tonight.

ETA for LA is roughly 9am.

3:25am

I hit a Texas speed bump. The little armadillo is the first road kill of the Trip.

Poor little guy.

I tried my hardest to miss him but I was going 80 and I didn't see him until it was too late to veer. Sorry, armadillo, but I don't want to roll the Vanbino.

In the seconds before impact, I figured his best chance of survival would be for me to try and glide over him and hope that he'd be lucky enough to clear the height of the space between the bottom of the Vanbino and the road.

He was not lucky enough. There was a loud thud on the front bumper and then the scraping sound as the underbelly of the Vanbino ravaged his helpless body. I looked back through the rear-view mirror and saw a battered carcass in several pieces fly out from under us and scatter across the highway.

Poor little guy.

4:30am

As I pulled into a rest stop in the middle of the Arizona desert, my headlights illuminated a sign right in front of me – 'AVISO' it said with a picture of a rattlesnake. I thought about it for a second. I looked through the windshield. It's pitch dark out there. So I just opened the door and urinated while still sitting in the seat. Rattlesnakes blend into the ground and you can barely see them in daylight so no way was I stepping foot outside in the dark.

6:05am

We are crossing through the Sierra Mountains (I think…) in the San Fernando Valley. Finally some different scenery! The sky is beginning to lighten behind us and after 2,182 miles, we are leaving I-10.

Farewell I-10, it's been fun... NOT!

I grew up with a girl named Carrie and because our families lived next door, we did everything together. One of the first pictures of either one of us is of both of us as infants sitting together on the couch. She is my oldest friend and she is one of my best friends and she remains so to this day. Carrie now lives in Hollywood off Wilshire Boulevard.

As we pulled up in front of her apartment, she was waiting outside on the front step. I hadn't seen her in several months since she moved and it felt good to hug her again.

Tom is also here. He flew out a couple days ago and has been staying with Carrie. He's going to the Dodgers game with us today and the Angels game tomorrow and then I think the plan is to meet back up with him in San Fran on Wednesday.

"I hit an armadillo last night," I told them as they came up to greet us.

"Oh shit!" Tom said.

"I tried to give it a chance to sneak under but it didn't make it."

"I hit a baby rabbit once," Tom told us. "It, like, hopped right out in front of me and I didn't see it till the last second and I wasn't sure if I even hit it or not. So I turned around and went back and it was lying there in the road like half dead trying to crawl away. I didn't know what to do so I ran over it again. I felt bad." He looks around at each one of us for some support on his decision. This was obviously a questionable move at the time and something that's been plaguing his morals. "I didn't want him to suffer, you know?"

"I would have done the same thing man," I said and patted him on the back.

Carrie had her head inside the side door of the van to see the chaos firsthand. She started laughing, "Oh my God the van smells like shit," Carrie said backing out and waving a hand in front of her nose.

"Really?" I said smelling it. It smelled fine to me.

"It's bad," she said nodding her head.

I uncovered the always-available Febreze from the glove compartment and sprayed it around inside. "There we go. All better."

Carrie rolled her eyes and walked inside where a fresh pot of coffee waited for us.

"You probably don't want any now, do you? You want to take a nap before the game?" Carrie asked.

"I'm actually not tired at all," I said somewhat surprised. I only managed two hours of sleep last night but I feel great right now. I feel like I could drive another 3,000 miles.

"What time's the game today?" Carrie asked.

"One. Are you coming?"

"I can't, I have class," Carrie said. "But I'm coming to the game tomorrow for sure."

"Good," I said. Tomorrow should be fun – a few days ago we got an email from Tailgate Magazine. They heard about our trip online and asked us if we'd be interested in them throwing a tailgate party for us when we're in Anaheim at the Angels game.

"Free food and free booze," Jay told us in his email. Without much hesitation, I said, "ummm, sure. I think we can manage that."

12:00pm

This is my first time in LA (my first time on the West Coast, for that matter) and the one thing I always hear about LA is the traffic, traffic, traffic. So we left early for Dodger Stadium – Carrie didn't live far but we wanted to be safe.

Tom, from the back seat, said, "dude, this van really smells like shit." I honestly don't smell it.

We pulled into Chavez Ravine and hiked the enormous expanse of parking lot to Dodger Stadium. The parking lot is like a freaking desert – you get lost out here, you die.

Just to the north on one of the hillside faces are the words 'THINK BLUE' in the style of the famous HOLLYWOOD sign and just beyond that lies the palm-lined ballpark. Dodger Stadium opened in 1962, and is currently

180

the third oldest Major League ballpark, behind only Fenway and Wrigley.

We get to see a rivalry game today between the Dodgers and Giants. This classic rivalry dates back to the days in New York and is one of the oldest and most storied rivalries in all of sports, so strong, in fact, that it stayed intact even after both teams moved 3,000 miles away in 1958.

2:15pm

We're sitting way up at the top, first base side. The sun is beating down on us but there is a nice breeze coming through so the heat is not so bad.

Joey is sitting a few rows in front of us, sprawled out over four seats and two rows, his sunglasses on, his flip-flops kicked, and looking like this place was made for him. He brought his Banana Boat with him and his skin glistens from the thick layer of oil that he has on.

"You gotta take advantage. This is prime time to bronze. Gotta maintain the glow for the babes, ya know?" I can see Joey living here in LA – he has a very California way about him and he could definitely handle LA. I guess the real question would really be, can LA handle Joey?

Dodger Stadium is great. It's very roomy and laid-back just a real nice place to take in a ballgame. I hate to say it but the famous Dodger Dog is nothing special. I mean, it's just a foot-long hotdog. I guess in the end, though, it's worth getting just to say you had one but, really nothing special.

We're just hanging at the Vanbino now, waiting for traffic to thin out a little in this massive parking lot. I thought the size was a little extreme when we got here but now I see why it's so big. We saw a great pitching performance today – Eric Stulz pitched a four hit, complete game shutout and the Dodgers won 8-0.

"Hey, Trav, I was thinking of getting a nice wide shot of the stadium from that hill…" Pedro points to the tallest one around. "I think we should climb it and get a nice shot of the park with the LA skyline in the background."

"I'm down. Let's do it," I said.

4:30pm

At the base of the mountain (or I guess more technically just a really huge hill, I don't think it's quite big enough to be called a mountain) I looked up. It's tall, steep at some parts, and I'm sure there are snakes in these here hills. The other three are already on their way up, though, so I followed behind.

30 minutes later…

Jesus, we're only half way up and I'm about to pass out. It's so hot and I'm sweating and my thighs hurt. Pedro is on a rampage, though – he's flying up this hillside! This can't be the first time he's climbed a mountain, no way. And there are a lot of little holes in the sandy dirt. Snake holes? Do snakes dig holes? Don't they just hide under rocks?

182

The peak is in sight. I'm dripping, panting, exhausted. My shirt is sticking to my skin and my face is on fire and Pedro looks like he hasn't even broken a sweat. I didn't realize what I was getting myself into when I agreed to this. It definitely didn't look this tall from the parking lot.

Then I hear a voice... a kid's voice? Am I hallucinating? Then more... and as I listen harder I start to hear music faintly playing somewhere... an accordion? I definitely hear an accordion. The kids are laughing. Where the hell is that coming from? I thought we were completely alone up here, entirely removed from civilization. There's no way there are kids up here.

"You hear that?" I ask to whoever's listening.

"Yeah. Kids..." Tom says trying to pinpoint the sound.

It's getting louder. Then a wiffle ball rolls down from that last little hill we have left to reach the peak and it stops at a weed by my foot. I stare at it for a moment until I hear a little voice –

"Little help?" I look up and at the top of the hill is a little boy peaking over. He wears a Dodgers cap and his hand is outstretched. I just stare back in disbelief, very confused. I just scaled the face of a mountain and I feel like I'm miles away from civilization but now here's this little kid. Where the hell did this kid come from and how the hell did he get up here?

I throw the ball back and he runs off. As I climb the rest of the way and pull my body up onto the summit, I am suddenly thrown into a Mexican fiesta – balloons, banners, flags, grills, food, picnic tables decorated with streamers and brightly colored cloths, and a mariachi band plays to the crowds of people who are singing and dancing and having the time of their lives.

I mean this is literally a Mexican fiesta... on the top of a mountain... What the hell? No way did all these people scale the mountain like we just did...

Then I notice the cars in the parking lot behind the party. It is connected to a road that must run down the other side of the mountain. Hmm, shit... missed that road... would have made things a little easier...

In a sandy lot surrounded by some large boulders, a sandlot game of wiffle ball was going on. The three of us sat on one of those rocks watching the game. It was great – sandlot baseball against the backdrop of Dodger Stadium. We could not have planned it better and this is just another little example of how the little surprises along the way – meeting Ball in the House in Boston, the people at the tailgates, the sunset behind Tiger Stadium – are turning out to be the most memorable parts of the Trip.

Carrie calls my phone. "Where are you guys?" she says through static.

"On top of a mountain at some Mexican fiesta... let me call you back in a bit, okay? I'm getting terrible reception up here." I didn't realize how random that sounded until later when Carrie asked about it.

Before heading back down the mountain, the kids invited us to join in their game and we happily obliged. No way was I going to pass up some swings of the bat.

Carrie lives near the Grove so tonight we walked through there on our way to the Farmer's Market... which is AMAZING! They have everything there – anything you want, you can find. Fresh fruits and veggies, Mexican, Chinese, fish, steak, pizza, pasta... I mean literally everything.

Carrie and I got some Mexican food and I had an horchata for the first time (a milky, sweet rice drink). I guess that fiesta put me in the mood.

Woke up bright and early on this Mother's Day and called my mom from the side porch.

"You remembered!" my mom shouted into my ear. "Your brother said you were going to forget. He was expecting to move up to the "Favorite Son" spot."

"He's a douche, Mom. That's what douches do," I informed her in case she didn't know that that's what douches do.

Today would be a good day – we have the Angels game at 1:00 but before that, we have that Tailgate Magazine Tailgate in the Big A parking lot. Then after the game, Carrie is taking us to Venice Beach. I'm planning on letting loose a little today since we don't have any driving and tomorrow is only a short five-hour jump to Phoenix.

"Look for the Big A," I told Tom from behind the wheel as we pulled into Angels Stadium. He's in the passenger seat, eyes peeled. It shouldn't be that hard... I mean, it *is* called the "Big" A.

"There!" Tom points and the Big A appeared through my windshield as we turned a corner. Originally located inside the park to hold the scoreboard when the stadium first opened in '66, it was moved to the parking lot when the stadium was expanded to accommodate the Rams in the late 70's. The Angels have contemplated moving it back but decided against it since it has become a landmark along the Orange Freeway.

"Okay, now there should be a school bus. The tailgate guy said you can't miss it."

"School bus!" Tom shouts. Jay the Tailgate Guy was right – we couldn't miss it. The school bus is currently under several renovations to turn it into the "ultimate tailgate party bus." Its seats are ripped out and in their place is now a cabana bar and classic tailgating games like Washers and Cornhole.

"Welcome to sunny California," Jay welcomed us as we walked up, shook hands, and met his family. "Glad you guys made it."

"We are too," Joey said.

"This is the Ultimate Tailgate Party Bus," Jay said beaming with pride at his creation. "It's gonna make the rounds to every NFL stadium this season then finish in Miami at the Super Bowl. There's still a lot of work to do but you can see where we're headed with it. You guys hungry? Grab a beer."

The beer was a nice microbrew out of San Diego fittingly called Tailgate Beer. "We have some chicken fajitas and some beef fajitas, a nice Southern Cal tradition," Jay said stirring the food on the grill. I can tell this guy lives for tailgating... he even once tailgated the Jeopardy show.

"Alex Trebek join you?" Joey asked.

"Unfortunately, no," Jay answered.

12:30pm

We didn't buy tickets to this game in advance because I didn't think it would be sold out.

I was wrong.

At the ticket window, the cheapest seats they had available were $65 ones and they weren't even together. Since Carrie drove herself, she just decided to go to the beach and we would meet her there after the game. But we still had to find four tickets.

One of the guys we met at the tailgate had two extra and he gave them to us for nothing. This guy shared some stories of his childhood with us about what it was like growing up as a Cardinals fan in the Midwest in the 50's. His family didn't have a TV but they had a radio, and he remembers listening to Harry Caray and Jack Buck every night.

"To this day I listen to the radio," the man says. "Never the TV. The radio for me is more personal, more intimate. I listened to Harry and Jack every night for years – I grew up with them in my home and they became the sound of summer for me, the sound of baseball. Even though I never met them they felt like friends." He thinks about that for second then chuckles and looks up at me. "Kinda weird, isn't it? But I'm sure you felt the same way about Harry."

I nodded, knowing exactly what he's talking about.

"You listen to someone every day for six, seven months out of the year, you're gonna feel like you know them. That's just the way it is. And it's why the off-season is so hard because it's like your friends are going away. But then April comes and your friends are back and it's a beautiful reunion!"

I thanked him for the tickets and his stories and we headed for the park. How great are these fans? Everywhere we go, every city we're in, the fans continue to surprise us because they just genuinely want to help us – they talk with us, they feed us, they give us their extra tickets instead of trying to sell them. They open up to us about baseball and how it is a part of their life and they share stories from their childhood with us. One thing baseball fans all seem to have in common is a willingness to open up and tell their stories… and every story is different… every story has a new perspective on the game.

We still needed two more tickets.

We found a scalper who wanted to sell us two for $30.

"20," I said.

"25."

"Good," and I handed him the cash.

We entered through the main gate underneath the large helmets, bats, and balls that decorated the entranceway. The Angels were owned by Disney (and maybe they still are?) so I'm kind of expecting this park to have some of that Disney flare around.

Since our seats are not together and the park is full, we're just going to walk around. The Royals are here today and this will be the fourth or fifth time we've seen them. I swear we're not following them.

"I just realized," Pedro started, "The Los Angeles Angels literally means 'The The Angels Angels'." And he shakes his head.

We got a delicious nacho and cheese platter and found a spot at a terrace bar out in the right field pavilion to watch the game. With a rock waterfall in the shape of an "A" in center and all the ushers wearing turn-of-the-century red and white striped uniforms, I was right about some Disney flare here. But Disney is also known for their magic and there was some of that on the field today.

It was top of the ninth, Angels up 4-3 and Miguel Olivo at the plate. He swings and hits a bomb to deep left-center. Hunter sprints about 150 feet and leaps mid-stride… and snags the ball about a foot over the fence. The amazing catch not only stole a home run from Olivo but saved the game for the Angels. Hunter called it the second best catch of his career and he proved that there really are angels in the outfield here in Anaheim.

From Angels Stadium we went straight to Venice Beach to meet Carrie. We played Frisbee and swam in the freezing Pacific then headed to a Mexican cantina just off the dunes for some happy hour margaritas.

Pedro offered to be the DD and so for the rest of us, things went downhill pretty quickly. He bought Carrie and I a Red Devil shot (which I had never heard of) and we took it. It knocked both of us down. Why I'd ever want to put anything called a Red Devil in my body I'll never know.

Never again.

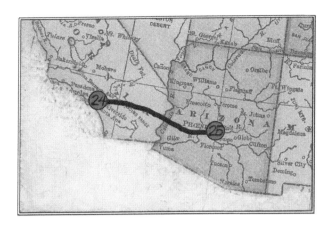

After the 3,000 mile marathon drive across the country a couple days ago, the five-hour trip to Phoenix seemed like a drive around the block. Joey and I were both hurting this morning, though, so Pedro took the wheel.

"Thanks for the Red Devils," I told him from behind my sunglasses. He just laughed and seemed to be enjoying my pain.

We first heard from Bob two weeks ago through email but didn't officially meet face to face until Phoenix. Like us, Bob is doing a ballpark tour of his own this year – he's seeing all thirty in one season – but unlike us, he's doing it for a cause. Bob recently and suddenly lost his wife from a heart condition known as SADS. Not much is known

193

about it and it's almost impossible to detect until it's too late. Bob is doing his ballpark tour to raise awareness of the disease.

A little before five, we walked into Slider's Bar right across from Chase. Bob was already there at a table with a beer. When he saw us walk in he stood up and greeted us with a huge smile.

"Guys, nice to finally officially meet you!" We've been talking regularly through email for the last two weeks and this did not feel like our first meeting; we have a lot in common and conversation was easy to come by. He bought us a round of beers and we shared stories from the road and about baseball.

"You guys are the ones who keep me going, you know that? You guys are my inspiration. I'm going to all thirty but I'm flying to them... you guys are *driving*... and in a month!" He laughs and takes a swig of his Shiner beer.

"Yeah but we're doing it just to do it. You actually have an important reason for doing it," I tell him.

"Shawn and I... really our relationship was founded on baseball. She was a Yankees fan and I was a Red Sox fan and we had fun with that but it was baseball, that common passion, that really united us." He paused. I could see Bob had more to say so we sat there and waited for him to talk.

"Shawn had a dog she named Jeter," through a reminiscing smile, "and after Shawn passed, Jeter went downhill pretty quickly. He just wasn't the same dog without her around and it wasn't long before he died from bloat. I buried him in the backyard. At Yankee Stadium you can buy a little bag of seeds of the kind of grass that they use on the field. So I bought a couple bags and planted one at Shawn's grave and one at Jeter's," Bob said with a smile. I can see he was proud of himself and had no reservations that that is exactly what Shawn would have wanted. "Shawn would have really liked that," he said smiling.

A long moment of silence ensues. "I'm glad you guys are doing this trip. I always talk about the Regret Fence, you know? If you have the opportunity to do something and aren't sure if you should do it, which way are you gonna go? You could take the safe way and not do it but always wonder 'what if' or you could take the adventure and do it. Maybe it's not the smartest idea but at least you can look back and say 'yeah, I did that.' At least you won't have any 'what-ifs.' I tend to go with the latter side."

There's a rhythm in Bob's words. He has a melodic way of speaking that is pleasant to listen to and I could sit here and listen to his stories for hours. His eyes are always smiling and are always warm, welcoming, and he has a certain way of making you feel comfortable around him.

"And that's really why I'm doing what I'm doing. I had the opportunity to do this kind of a trip and I took it. And what's funny is that I'm finding that it's not really about the ballparks anymore… they're great to see but it's become more about the experiences along the way then the ballparks themselves. Kind of like you guys and the wiffle ball game at the Dodgers park or Joey in the puma costume." Bob laughs. "It's those funny little experiences along the way that are really making the memories."

I nodded – I know exactly what Bob is talking about. He summed up what we've known since Day 1 and I could not have said it better myself.

"Anyway, have fun driving tomorrow because until you hit the Rockies, there's nothing," Bob says, chuckling, and he finishes off his Shiner.

Not only did Bob treat us to a couple rounds of beer at Slider's, but he bought us tickets to the D-Backs game, and not only did he buy us tickets to the D-Backs game, but he bought us tickets to an all-you-can-eat *suite* at the D-Backs game.

"I figured you guys might be hungry," Bob said.

Before leaving, I wrapped several hotdogs up in napkins and stuffed them in the pockets of my cargo shorts. Don't judge.

We also tried to go swimming in the pool that Chase has out in left but the security guard wouldn't allow it. Joey tried to grease him but still he refused.

"Not even for 20 bucks," Joey said surprised. "What's the deal?"

I'm in the back seat of the Vanbino looking over the box scores of the games we've seen. Joey is driving and Pedro is sleeping in the passenger seat. The faint, yellow light on the ceiling above my head is the only light in the cabin – we are in the middle of nowhere right now. No street lights, no passing cars… just darkness and the hum of the motor.

"I gotta get some new music," Joey said. "I think I've listened through my iPod like 16 times."

"We've been seeing a lot of high scoring games," I reported. "10-2 White Sox win in Chicago, 10-3 Cards over Cubs in St. Louis, 13 runs by the Bo-Sox in Boston and now 13 runs again tonight by the Reds."

"Yeah, the lowest scoring game, I think, was the 2-0 one in Cleveland," Joey said.

And tomorrow is Coors and we all know how the ball jumps out at Coors.

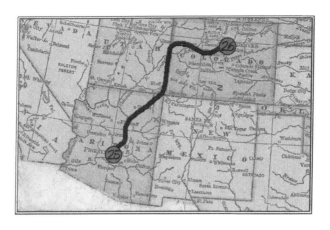

Tuesday, May 12 — DAY 25
Denver
7:05 Game @ Coors Field (Ballpark #26)
Total Miles Today — 821
Total Miles So Far — 10,791

6am

      Well, Bob was right about this drive – there's *nothing*. We stopped somewhere off State Road 191 in Utah to catch a little sleep. The last signs I saw were for a city named Moab… that doesn't really help pinpoint where we are, though, cause I've never heard of it. Joey and Pedro tag-teamed the drive tonight since I drove from LA to Phoenix.

Back on the road after a nice little nap – six hours on I-70 E and it will take us through the Rockies and straight into Denver. I'm excited to see the Rockies – this'll be my first time and I've heard nothing but how nice the park is.

We rolled into downtown Denver with plenty of time to spare before our 7:05 game at Coors tonight. In 12 days since our last oil change, we've driven the Vanbino just shy of 8,000 miles and tonight into tomorrow we'd be driving another 1,300 miles to get to San Francisco. Needless to say, she's due for another tune-up so we stopped at a Jiffy Lube.

After the tune-up, we freshened up in the parking lot – brushed our teeth, reapplied deodorant, etc. Pedro wrote a postcard to Krystal that he had picked up in LA. I tried reading it over his shoulder but he wrote it in Spanish.

The cheapest general admission tickets for Coors are $4 for the Rockpile section out in center field. We got those and as we sit out in the bleachers (that we have almost all to ourselves) I look up and notice the ring of purple seats that circles through the otherwise black-seated ballpark. That row marks one mile above sea level, making Coors Field the highest elevated ballpark in the Majors. (And interestingly enough, we just came from the second highest ballpark – Chase Field. I would not have guessed that).

This ballpark has a neat story – everybody knows the high altitude in Colorado makes for dry, thin air but nobody knew exactly how this would affect the flight of the baseball. It was assumed that the ball would fly further so this park was designed and built with unusually large field dimensions to compensate. When it opened, the theories proved to be true and, despite it being one of the largest parks in the Majors, it gave up record-breaking home run numbers in its first couple of years. Tests were done and it was concluded that it was more the dryness of the air than the thinness of the air affecting the flight of the baseball. So, prior to the '02 season, a humidor was installed where the game balls would be stored in a wetter environment, therefore making them heavier. The humidor worked and brought home run tallies down to a consistent level with other ballparks.

Anyway, on the diet front (I'm actually dreading what I'm going to have to eat here at Coors in just a few minutes) I've been doing great since my physical breakdown in Milwaukee last week. I haven't been eating as much fast food (except for when I see a Jack In the Box… it's impossible for me to drive past one and not get something). I've been doing "grocery shopping" at gas stations and just getting little things like bread and yogurt and fresh fruit and all. That little change has made a big difference and overall, I'm feeling much more energized and much more alert.

But here we are now in Colorado and my diet is about to take another hit – not quite in terms of cholesterol intake but in terms of bizarreness – and I'm not sure if I'm going to be able to stomach this, to be honest.

The Rocky Mountain Oysters at Coors are not really oysters, per se… they are bull testicles, sliced up and deep fried and served in a paper tray with a side of fries.

Mmmm… bull balls. I'm not too keen on trying bull balls but I have to – whatever it takes, right? And, plus, on the bright side, the line to get them is long and I see a lot of people walking around with the snack and popping them like they're potato chips. So how bad can they be…?

7:20pm

We're sitting back at our Rockpile seats now after getting an order. I hold the generous helping of Rocky Mountain Oysters out in front of me, staring down at them, apprehensive and unsure, not really too eager to dig in. They look like fried zucchini except more gray, and… more testicle-like.

Joey rips a testicle chip in half and examines the inside. It's stretchy and elastic like, like… flesh.

"Bon appétit." Joey pops one in and chews it. Swallows it. Doesn't say anything. Anticipation mounts.

"Well?" Pedro asks after a long moment.

After some hesitation, Joey picks up his beer and responds. "Tastes like what a freaking scrotum would probably taste like." He chugs his Dos Equis.

"That's not just scrotum, though, that's ball," Pedro clarifies.

I go ahead and pop one in fast and chew it. I try to swallow it but I gag – actually gag – and I'm barely able to get it down. I'm picky with the textures of my food and this texture was definitely not good. I chugged my Dos Equis.

"You like it, Trav?" Pedro asks. I just look at him, barely able to breathe and hardly able to chew – this was one of the most vile things I have ever eaten. What I would give for a Jack In the Box burger and tots right now.

Pedro pops a big one and chews it. He nods his head in agreement and he swallows no problem.

"Not bad," he says as he reaches for another.

8:15pm

We couldn't stay long at Coors. Tonight is our longest drive and we have the shortest amount of time to do it in. We have a 1:35 game tomorrow in San Francisco – 1,300 miles away and only 17 hours to get there. The Babe is giving us an ETA of 4:35pm so tonight we'll stop *only* for gas and nothing else. We have a bunch of empty Gatorade bottles lying around the Vanbino that we may have to reuse…

This drive has been "The One"… "The One" that has been looming over our heads, taunting us with the very real notion that it could very well be our undoing. If one thing goes wrong tonight (traffic, flat tire, *anything*…) we're done. The Trip could end here. The ambition-stupidity line is present in my mind – this drive will really clarify which side we're on.

Pedro and his lead foot are taking the first leg. He'll take us north out of Denver and into Wyoming then once we hit Cheyenne, we'll jump on I-80 W to take us back out to the coast.

Pedro and his lead foot...

"Is that for me?" Pedro asked looking at the cop car tailing him in the rear-view mirror.

"Of course it is," I tell him. "We're the only ones out here."

"Shit! I wasn't even going that fast!"

"You were going pretty fast," I say.

Pedro slows and pulls to the shoulder. The cop follows. He throws his hands up in the air in frustration. "Why doesn't Joey get a ticket?!"

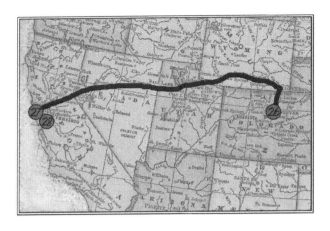

Wednesday, May 13 — DAY 26
Doubleheader Day #5 — San Francisco & Oakland
1:35 Game @ AT&T Park (Ballpark #27)
7:35 Game @ Oakland Coliseum (Ballpark #28)
Total Miles Today — 1,270
Total Miles So Far — 12,061

2:30am

It's 2:30am and we're out of gas. We're somewhere in Wyoming and we've been on "E" for a good 20 minutes. There's nothing…. I mean, nothing. There aren't even any exits. How far can cars run on fumes? Isn't it 30 miles or something? We're completely screwed if we run out of gas. I have AAA but it'll probably take them days to reach us out here. How are there no exits??? This is a highway!

I search for the closest gas station on the Babe. It says there's one five miles up the road. Pedro floors it. I've been drifting in and out of sleep for the past couple of hours but I haven't even seen one car out here. This is weird.

Five miles up the road, the exit sign is like a God-send. That familiar, bright chrome green color of the highway sign is a beautiful sight. But as we reach the gas station we pull up beside it and our hearts sink. We are speechless. A tall medal fence surrounds the perimeter of the gas station and stops us from going any further than the curb. There are giant holes and mounds of dirt beneath the canopy where the pumps should be and there's a tiny sign on the fence just to our left that laughs in our faces – "Pardon Our Appearance."

Pardon Our Appearance?? Really???!! This was literally the first gas station in 100 miles and it's closed??!! I almost flipped but I had to keep my cool – we have no time to waste.

The Babe says there's another one ten miles more down 80. Is there enough sludge in the tank to get us there? This one has to be open... right?

Ten miles down the highway we take the next exit, this time a lot less optimistic, and pull into the gas station. No fence around this one but no lights on either. It's pitch dark, empty...

"Is it open?" Pedro asks as he pulls up to a pump.

From the back, Joey answers, "no, it's not open. What are you stupid?"

"Can we still use the pumps?"

"No… the little lady in there has to push a button inside or something. It's closed. We're screwed," Joey says. "Game over."

The one light – the only sign of life on the vacant property – comes from the little meter window on the gas pump. "Well we gotta try," I say getting out.

I slide our debit card into the payment slot on the pump… and we wait… and we wait… and we wait for what seems like an hour.

Finally a beep and then the illuminated screen switches to say 'PLEASE SELECT FUEL GRADE.' I quickly push UNLEADED and stick the nozzle in the Vanbino and squeeze the handle. Nothing for a long moment and then, all at once, the fuel begins to flow like the water over Niagara and the numbers on the meter quickly flicker up as it calculates our bill.

"Oh thank God!" Pedro exclaims into the Wyoming night. I laugh in relief along with him and as I stand by the pump, I realize for the first time how *freaking* cold it is. A strong wind blows and having just come from 90 degrees in Denver, I'm still in shorts and a tee-shirt.

5:35am

It's just about daybreak and as the eastern sky begins to lighten, I notice the flat ground that surrounds the highway slowly begin to change from green to white.

"I'm getting tired," I thought. "I've been driving since the gas fiasco." In an effort to refresh my sight, I close my eyes for a brief moment then take a sip of my lemon lime Gatorade and reach for the sunflower seeds.

I exhale and continue my stare into the overwhelming monotony that the highway is so good at providing. Even though dawn is upon us, the moon still hangs high in the sky and it casts a heavy glow upon the surrounding, flat, white plains and they appear to be glowing.

"What the hell is going on out there?" I know we can't afford to stop but I have to see what this is – this is too weird.

I park the Vanbino on the shoulder and get out. The stop wakes Joey and he follows me out onto the glowing white ground. It's spongy, hard to the touch but soft when you walk on and is crackly, looking like it could crumble beneath our feet at any moment.

"It's the Salt Flats," Joey yells to me over the heavy wind. This is amazing – for as far as the eye can see in all directions, a glowing white ground. The wind is whipping out here and it is absolutely freezing. I thought the temp might feel a bit exaggerated because of the summer attire I'm in but when I got back into the Vanbino I checked. Nope – 37 degrees. Holy shit.

7:30am

We just crossed the border into Nevada and we still have about 10 hours of driving ahead of us. We have eight hours until first pitch.

Thanks to Pedro, we've been making good time so far and all we can hope for now is to keep on our current pace.

9:30am

"Nevada sucks, man. Jesus," I say. This is worse than the drive through Florida... maybe even worse than the drive through Texas. I feel like we've been driving in circles forever because the scenery never changes. At least there's nobody around so we can piss outside instead of in a bottle.

1:35pm

Earlier, we drove through beautiful snow-covered mountains in Lake Tahoe and are now passing through Sacramento. It's time for first pitch at AT&T Park and we're still one and a half hours away. Pray for no traffic.

2:45pm

I can see the Golden Gate Bridge sitting in some heavy fog way off in the distance as we drive along water. My mind and body feel numb from this drive and I feel like just a shell of myself.

On top of this drive, we have a doubleheader day today (our last one) – first game in San Fran then a nightcap across the Bay in Oakland.

We are close, though... so very, very close...

3:05pm

As soon as Joey parked the Vanbino, I jumped out and began sprinting the good quarter mile to the ballpark. For all I knew the game was in the 9th inning…

I think it's safe to say that I'm out of shape because the sprinting only lasted about a quarter of a quarter of a quarter mile. I slowed into a brisk walk and then by the time I reached AT&T I was pretty much crawling. I guess I have a reputation for not "being in shape" because when I saw Tom waiting by the gate for me, he was laughing. Joey and Pedro had caught up to me and now only trailed a few paces behind me.

"I told this kid to get in shape before the trip!" Tom yelled to them. Then looking at me, "don't worry, man, it's only the top of the 6th. You made it!"

3:35pm

Sitting in our seats, lower level, third base side. Zimmerman has a 30-game hit streak on the line today – so far he is 0 for 2.

I'm eating a beef-kabob and some garlic fries and drinking a Prohibition Ale (which I really only got because I like the name). All we've been hearing about are the famous garlic fries here so we had to get them. They lived up to the hype – and they even come with a mint!

"Here." Pedro hands me my inhaler. I have asthma and that dash to the ballpark really knocked me on my ass.

"Dude... thanks." It meant a lot to me that Pedro had thought enough to grab my inhaler for me... cause I sure as hell hadn't.

Zimmerman ended the day 0 for 3 and so his streak came to an end at 30. Our quest to 30, however, remained intact. We played some ball on the Little League field beside our Ballpark #27 before heading out; Oakland is only 30 minutes from here across the Bay Bridge so we have some time to kill before the 7:05 game tonight.

What to say about AT&T... well, I guess I'll start by saying that it's been one of my favorite parks I've been to so far. In terms of the scenery, the intimacy, and the food and the beer menus, the Giants home is truly something special. Towards the end of the game, we had sat out in right field beside the bay. There was one lonely kayaker sitting on the water and if a splash homer had been hit today, the ball would have been as good as his.

Joey pitched the ball to Pedro, who swung and missed. "That was my curve," Joey told him. I was behind home plate and I threw the ball back to Joey. "Watch out. Here comes my heater."

From a design point of view, AT&T is an interesting park because it revisits the original plan of early ballpark construction. Like all of the early ballparks from the 1910's and 20's, the shape of this park was dictated entirely by the plot of land it stands on, just like Fenway and Wrigley were. Baseball started in the fields but when its popularity began to boom and owners began to charge money to watch teams play, the game moved into the cities. The owners only had a certain sized plot of land to build their parks on and so to fit them into cramped city blocks, asymmetrical fields were necessary. Same thing goes for AT&T Park – the Giants didn't have much space to build, so the compensation for this is what gives the park its funky outfield dimensions and that 25-foot brick wall in right. For me, the asymmetrical field is one of the things that makes baseball great and what really attracts me to the sport. The fact that every field is a different shape and size is unique to the sport of baseball – every football field is 360x160, every basketball court is 94x50, every hockey rink 200x85, but from city to city, team-to-team, every baseball field is different. I know for some this is unfair and is one of the problems with baseball but I think this is one of its great strengths. Not only does it add more strategy to each and every game, but it adds more strategy to the actual *building* of a team, as well.

AT&T is a true throwback and a genuine nod to the ballparks of yesteryear.

6:00pm

"Hey, man, you hear from Bartels?" I asked Tom from the back seat.

"Yeah, he just texted me and said he's taking the train from work and should be there by game time."

Bartels is another old friend of Tom and mine from the neighborhood growing up and he moved out to San Francisco after college. We're all crashing at his place tonight.

212

"It's small, man," Bartels warned about his apartment. "Like you're-gonna-have-to-cuddle-with-Tom small."

"Fine by me," I told him. "No big deal – Tom and I are close."

6:20pm

I didn't buy tickets for the A's game because I knew we wouldn't have a problem getting them, but this is ridiculous! Not only is it Dollar Dog Night tonight at the Coliseum, but it's Dollar *TICKET* Night, as well... and the place is *STILL* empty! What the hell!! They literally cannot *give* tickets away. It's a shame but the Coliseum for baseball sucks. I know the A's are trying to get a new ballpark and I really hope it happens for them sometime soon.

I'm always weary of Dollar Dog Nights because I had a bad experience at one in Philly a couple years ago. It was the first Dollar Dog Night I had ever been to and I got a little carried away with it. I ate eleven hotdogs on that fateful night, left the game early with a stomachache, went home and threw up for two hours. It was the worst and ever since then, I've given myself a two-hotdog cap. But everyone else is taking full advantage and going to town.

There's been a guy in an elephant costume walking around the Coliseum all night. "What's the deal with the elephant?" I ask Joey.

"It's their mascot... the white elephant," Joey answered with a mouthful of hotdog.

"You got some mustard on your lip." I motion at it with my finger.

"I get it?"

I re-inspect. "Yeah, you're good."

I found out later where the White Elephants came from – way back in the day when the A's were still in Philly, the New York Giants then-manager John McGraw called the team "a white elephant." The A's embraced it and the rest is history.

11:30pm

I tried describing Bartels to Joey and Pedro before they met him but it was useless. He's a unique character, beats his own drum and it's impossible to get to know him without meeting him face-to-face. His apartment is decorated with framed, autographed headshots of Gary Coleman, Jerry Stiller and Gary Busey; standing up behind his DVD collections of gory, B-rated horror films and standup comedy acts is a record LP with Murphy Brown's face on the cover and beside that, a VHS of Mr. Bean and Jack Benny; and then there's the centerpiece of the room – an expensive vodka held in a clear bottle in the shape of a skull. This is not just any vodka, though… it is vodka that is distributed by Dan Aykroyd himself… and this is an autographed bottle.

I realized that Bartels wasn't joking about me having to cuddle with Tom tonight. And, judging by the size of it, I may be cuddling with Joey and Pedro, too.

When we got back to his place, we had every intention of going out and exploring San Fran a little... so much easier said than done. Bartels had one of his favorite movies "Windy City Heat" on and I made the mistake of sitting down on the couch.

I did not get back up.

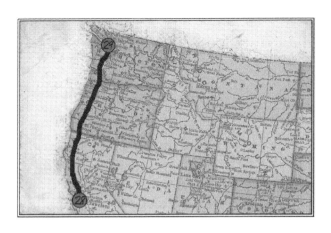

I woke up in the same position I fell asleep in last night – sitting up on the couch with the remote in my hand – and I did not wake up once. The only other time I slept sitting up was in a wooden rocking chair watching "Amityville Horror" at a sleepover in 8th grade... oh yeah, and a couple weeks ago in Boston.

"This van really smells like shit," Bartels says as he climbs into the back seat.

"Does it?" I ask.

"Yeah," Tom quickly answers for him.

217

It still smells fine to me.

On one of those long drives a couple nights ago, we stopped at some trucker rest stop and Joey picked up an air freshener. It was a plastic slice of watermelon, personified with big goofy eyes, dangling legs, and it was holding something green in its hands. I unwrapped it from the package.

"What's it smell like?" Joey asks me.

I take a whiff then shrug when I come to the obvious answer… "watermelon." I hang it on the rear view mirror.

"It does smell like watermelon," he agrees.

The next couple of days will be a nice change of pace for us. Although Seattle is over 800 miles and 14 hours away, the game isn't until tomorrow night at 7:00. We have some time this morning and Bartels took us on a little sightseeing tour of San Fran. We drove the Vanbino down the famous winding Lombard Street, walked around Fisherman's Wharf, saw the seals on the pier and Alcatraz Island in the Bay then went down to the Golden Gate Bridge and had a catch in the park that sits beside it.

The tour was capped off at Buena Vista Café, home of the original Irish Coffee and damn are they good! This place serves up to 2,000 of them *a day*! Unreal.

8pm

Not sure exactly where we are – somewhere on I-5 in northern California.

"Bigfoot territory," Joey announced.

Pedro has had no problem sleeping in the van and he's passed out in the back. Tom stayed in San Fran with Bartels and the plan is to pick him back up on our way down to San Diego in a few days.

"That thing really does smell like watermelon," Joey says from the passenger seat. He's right – the Vanbino is now overwhelmingly full with the stench of artificial watermelon. It's pretty powerful for such a tiny little ornament. "What's it holding though?"

"I don't know." I was wondering that myself. "I think it's a cucumber."

"Why would a watermelon be holding a cucumber?" He looks at me like I'm insane.

"I don't know. What else could it be?"

"I think it's his rind."

"It's definitely not his rind," I say pointing to the back of the watermelon slice where his rind is. "Look."

Joey sees. "Somebody else's rind?"

"Why would he be holding somebody else's rind? That'd be like me holding your arm if it fell off."

Joey thinks hard about the whole situation for a long while then he gives up. "Maybe it *is* a cucumber... or a pickle. But a pickle *is* a cucumber, so..." he trails off in thought, then, "man, I can't remember the last time I had a pickle. I love pickles. So refreshing. You ever have a pickle back?"

I shake my head.

"Awww, dude! A shot of Jameson, right, then a shot of pickle juice as a chaser. Dude… unreal," Joey says emphatically.

When you've spent as much time on the road as we have, you find things to talk about and every topic seems interesting. Also when you're on the road, you have a lot of time to think.

I'm not sure where or when it happened but constantly moving from one place to another has become our normal day. We're used to it now – nomadic has become our new way of life and the road has become our home. At the beginning, a six, seven, eight hour drive was brutal – and I dreaded them – and I remember thinking then how in the world would I survive the long drives out west? These kinds of day-long drives seemed insurmountable back then.

But now, two weeks later, I don't even think about it; in fact, I actually even welcome the driving. A 14-hour drive, a 20-hour drive is nothing. It might sound weird but I almost feel at ease on the road, empowered even, like I am in complete control of everything. Nothing can touch me out here; nothing can hold me down. It's freedom in its rawest form.

I look through my mirror at Pedro, who is awake now. His head still rests on the seat, slumped to one side, but his eyes are open and he stares out the window into nothing in particular. I know he is thinking about Krystal. He misses her much more than he has let on.

I glance over at Joey. He, too, stares out the window and his eyes have that same distant look as Pedro's. He's talked a lot lately about how much there is out there to see. He feels like he's been missing a lot being holed-up in his little studio apartment above the cheese steak shop in South Philly and now he's finally realizing just how much he *is* missing. If nothing else, this Trip has opened his eyes.

The beautiful scenery of mountains, rivers, and conifer forest pass by their glazed eyes without them taking much notice of it. I think all the sleepless nights and busy days are catching up to us and exhaustion will not be staved off much longer. They're both lost in their thoughts... thoughts that I can see on the surface of their eyes. It's amazing how well we've gotten to know each other these past few weeks. We were friends before, yes... but not like this. This is more. This is deeper. We've gotten to know each other intuitively, psychologically... so well that we understand each other without a word having to be said. The three of us, and the three of us alone, have faced all the emotional and all the physical ups and downs a trip like this brings and together, we've overcome them. It's forged a strong bond between us and has made us as close as brothers.

I fumble around in the messy center consol between the front two seats for the bag of homemade beef jerky we picked up at a stop in Wyoming. "This shit is the best shit in the world," the toothless lady who sold it to us said. Normally my instincts would tell me not to buy food from her, but being tired and hungry, I was a little whacked and I did anyway.

My fumbling around snapped Joey from his thoughts. "What do you need?"

"Where's that jerky?" I ask.

"Oh… I ate it…" I heard from the back. I look at Pedro through the mirror and he's looking at me with a little sheepish smile. "There's a box of Mini Wheats," he offered.

"Are they frosted?"

"Yeah." He hands me a little box of Mini Wheats from the food trunk.

"Here take a juice, too. Travvy needs his vitamins," Joey said. He opens the straw and sticks it in the hole and hands it to me.

"Thanks, guys."

We parked at a little rest stop and walked around for a bit to stretch our legs. This scenery in the Pacific Northwest is just breathtaking – everywhere I look is a postcard.

"He's out here, I know it… and I'm gonna find him," I hear Joey say as he walks up behind me. He's talking about Bigfoot, of course. Before we left for the Trip, Joey saw a show on TV about finding evidence of Bigfoot in the Pacific Northwest and, much to Pedro and mine's chagrin, that's the only topic he's been discussing for the last day and a half.

12:30pm

"Ahoy!!" the fish man yelled just before throwing a fifteen pound, three foot long fish of some kind across the large icy tables full of all kinds of fish. Behind the counter,

Joey snagged it out of the air and holds it up like a trophy for the cheering crowd.

"That's been a dream of mine," he says stepping out from behind the counter of the famous Pike's Place Fish Market in downtown Seattle. He is all smiles but the front of his shirt is covered in a layer of slimy fish oil. Pedro laughs.

"Dude, you're gonna stink!" he tells Joey.

"Bigfoot bait," Joey says. "Watch out."

Before heading down to the Pyramid Ale House across from Safeco, we had some lunch at the Public Market and Joey had his first oyster shooter.

"Better than Rocky Mountain Oysters, I'll tell ya that," he said when I asked him if he liked it. He spilled some cocktail sauce on him in the process of taking it. Oh well – it'll go along with the stench of fish oil.

Speaking of stench… when was the last time I showered? I didn't have a chance at Bartels'... was it really five days ago in LA at Carrie's? Holy shit, that is disgusting if that's true. All the days are running together so I'm not exactly sure how accurate that is but that sounds about right. I've washed my face and pits at rest stops and all but that's about the extent of my hygiene maintenance. Oh, well… I'm not trying to impress anyone. That's life on the road, baby!

5:30pm

Craig and Ken met us at the Pyramid Ale House before the game. They are two die-hard ballpark chasers who make their home in Seattle. Craig is so into ballpark chasing, in fact, that he built a whole online community called ballparkchasers.com, sort of like a Facebook for ballpark chasers. They are both particularly interested in our ballpark tour because of the driving aspect of it.

Over beers, the five of us share our stories about our favorite ballparks, our least favorite, and those funny, random experiences from the road that Bob had talked about.

"Each park is so unique," Craig started. "I've had the pleasure of seeing about half of the current parks right now and what's amazing is each one has its own atmosphere."

"It's the total experience – it's not *just* the ballgame," Ken said. "I keep telling my wife that the ballgame is almost secondary to the experience of meeting people at the ballpark, the foods the beers... everything – just all the local flavors from around the country. No two ballparks are the same. There's a lot that are similar but no two are the same."

Craig nodded in agreement as he listened to Ken who met through Craig's website. "I chase ballparks and started the website because I love the stadiums and I love the games. If there's one thing I could do, it's going to catch a game at the ballpark. The smells, the sounds... just the atmosphere, the food, the fans that interact – it just makes for a great day."

"If I had my pick of any ballpark to be at, it'd be bleacher seats at Wrigley Field," Ken shared. "I mean, there's just so much energy, so much excitement... it's... there's something almost hair-raising at Wrigley, you know? It is a religious experience, most definitely."

I couldn't agree more.

I told them our story about finding the wiffle ball game on top of that mountain outside of Dodger Stadium. "It's funny," I say, "because after all the months of planning leading up to the Trip, the parts that stick out the most aren't the ballgames or the ballparks but the little surprises that we just happen to stumble upon along the way."

They understood.

Meeting Ken and Craig is another one of those pleasant little surprises.

8:15pm

We're way up high in Safeco but it doesn't matter – the view is amazing. Like Minute Maid and Miller, Safeco has a retractable roof, but unlike those parks, the roof acts more like an umbrella and the park is never fully enclosed. It happens to be a perfect night outside tonight and so the roof is open and I don't even notice it because it blends so seamlessly into the park.

The food here is definitely more sophisticated than the usual ballpark fare that we've grown so accustomed to. I have a salmon sandwich and some sushi, or, the Ichi-roll, as it's known at Safeco.

10:30pm

We saw the Mariners beat the Red Sox 5-4 tonight on the strength of two Ichiro home runs and saw Ellsbury miss the cycle by a home run. On the way out, we walked past a stand that sells chocolate covered fruit on a stick and so I got one.

Bad idea. The assembly of the fruit on the stick was as follows – a large, upside-down strawberry on the bottom, half a banana (point towards the top), and then another upside-down strawberry, this one smaller than the other. Take a second to picture that... Since the whole thing is dipped in chocolate, you could not make out the individual fruits and so it looked like one shape... one very phallic looking shape, if you will. Pedro and Joey were obviously having some fun with this.

"It's fruit. Jesus," I said with a mouthful of chocolate and banana.

Midnight

I watched Mount Ranier shrink in the rear view mirror as we retraced our route back down I-5. Tomorrow, we'd make a quick pit stop in San Fran to pick up Tom then continue south to LA where we'd spend tomorrow night at Carrie's. She is just two hours from San Diego so we'd push off early Sunday morning to make the 1:00 first pitch at Ballpark #30.

Ballpark #30.

I can't believe it. Has it really already been a month? When I think back on particular instances like the Sausage Guy on Lansdowne, the burnt ends in KC, meeting Bob in Phoenix, they seem like they happened months ago. But when I think about the Trip as a whole, all the driving we've done and the places we've visited, there's no way it's already been a month! It seems like we just started.

226

I sat next to a guy on an airplane once on my way back from Savannah to Philly. My first college trimester had finished and I was flying home for Thanksgiving. He was an older man, probably 70, 75 or so, with very kind eyes as if proof that he's satisfied and happy with the life he's led.

"I can't believe my first trimester is already done," I was telling him. "I feel like I just got to school."

He nodded his head and smiled like he knew all too well what I was talking about. "Time flies and the older you get, the faster it goes."

"That's disappointing," I say. "Is there anyway to slow it down?"

Then he leaned in close to me, looked me in the eye and spoke to me in a harsh whisper, "travel," he said, letting me in on his secret. "Never stop moving. Never stop because once you do you start dying." He spoke with so much conviction behind his words that I knew they were coming from his heart. Then after a moment he leaned back into his chair and said one more thing. "Age, time... is all just a perception. It's all just what you make it out to be."

I don't remember what else we spoke about on the flight that night but I found that bit of philosophy so poignant that, to this day, I think about it and the "older" I become, the more it appears to be true. I am convinced that that wise man – that random encounter I had on just another day – was a genius. I wonder where he is today, where his travels have taken him. Wherever he is, I have no doubt he is happy.

And now here I am, here *we* are, on the home stretch of our month-long marathon across the country.

But we're not there yet. We still have 1,300 miles left to drive and a lot can happen in 1,300 miles...

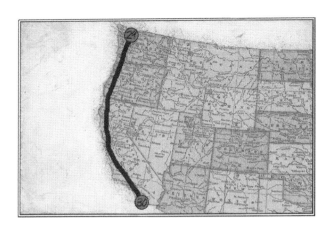

It was 9pm by the time we rolled into Carrie's. We walked up to the Farmer's Market again for dinner, then went back to Carrie's and drank on her porch for a while.

I know I should be tired but I'm wide awake. Either that or I'm so tired, that I'm mistaking delirium for alertness. Does that make sense? Whatever, I don't care. I'll sleep when I'm dead. I still know north from south and at this point that's all that matters. And these Pale Moons and Sam Summers are tasting pretty sweet right now.

Carrie woke me up and I jumped to look at a clock –
I had just dreamt that we had missed the game. She laughed.

"Relax," she said softly. "It's only seven. I'm going
to put a pot of coffee on. Do you want some eggs?"

"That would be great," I told her as I laid my head
back down on the pillow, exhaling a sigh of relief. Carrie's
following us down to San Diego today to (hopefully)
celebrate the completion of our quest.

By eight we were all up, showered (finally!!) and
were finishing up breakfast. Joey reported that traffic looked
fine and so by 8:45, we were packed and rolling out.

We're back on I-5 hugging the coast to San Diego.
There are over 15,000 miles of road in our rear view mirrors
and now there is just 120 miles standing between us and
fulfilling our quest. Even if the Vanbino breaks down now
I'm hitch-hiking. I don't care.

Nothing can stop us now…

10:12am

…except for rain. Black clouds have pushed out the
blue skies and raindrops start to splatter the windshield of
Vanbino. For the past week and half to two weeks, the
weather has been great and I wasn't even thinking about rain
today.

No way… not now. No way can our first rainout happen on our last day… and in sunny San Diego of all places! I didn't think it ever rains in San Diego…

Joey just looked this up: Petco didn't experience its first rainout until April of '06 – a full two years after it opened! Was all our good luck catching up with us? That would be cruel…

11am

It's 11am and I can see the San Diego skyline come into view through the windshield and blue, sunny skies are overhead. That's right – blue, sunny skies and not a cloud in sight!

We went to the Marriott that my mom had booked for us first to drop off our bags and check-in. The hotel is just a couple blocks from Petco so we'll just leave the Vanbino there and walk to the ballpark.

"Can you take my bag to the room, Trav?" Carrie asked me, handing it to me before I could say no. "I gotta go see something. I'll meet you at the park." And she left. You don't have to have known her for as long as me to see that she's obviously up to something.

11:45am

I step outside from the cool hotel lobby into the warm, San Diego sunshine. It's perfect right now – probably 82 degrees with a cool breeze coming off the Pacific and not a cloud in the sky; we could not have asked for a better day to wrap up the Trip.

I can see the ballpark from here, Petco Park... Ballpark #30... and Tom, Joey, Pedro, and I walk towards it. We know we are on the verge of accomplishing something special. For the last 30 days, we had devoted our lives to this journey, we set our sights on a goal and, despite the times and moments of despair and misfortune, we stuck with it, never deviated from the plan, and now we were about to be rewarded. The success of our goal was now within our reach – we could see it and we could feel it.

As I walked along the train tracks that run between Petco and the Marriott, I see a small group of people waving to us. There's Carrie and... who is she with? I look closer and see that it's my dad and Wes.

I don't believe it. I knew Carrie was up to something!

When I reached them, I hugged Wes and then my dad. I had no idea that they were going to be here with us and to join in the celebration of accomplishing a goal that they all had a hand in. What a great surprise!

"Mom has to work. She hates she couldn't make it," my dad told me. That's the only thing that could have made this better. But she's here in spirit.

At the gates, I handed my ticket to the usher and I walked through the turnstile. If this was a movie, this scene would be in slow-motion to play up the drama because it's official – seeing a game in all 30 Major League ballparks in 30 days by driving only is possible and we did it.

We did it.

Our quest is complete.

My dad treated us all to fish tacos and Stella's and we enjoyed them out in our seats in the left field bleachers.

"What an amazing park," I thought as I sat there. Joey was in the seat in front of me and, as if hearing my thought, turned around and said, "you know, I think this might be one of my favorite parks."

I couldn't agree more and probably the thing I like most about it is that there is a public park out in center field and since it is public, it remains open even if the Padres aren't playing. It's also got that laid-back southern California vibe and, I think for maybe the first time in a month, I was watching a ballgame truly relaxed. We had nowhere to be tomorrow, nowhere to be the day after that and the day after that. We had time for ourselves, didn't have to set an alarm, didn't have to stress over a deadline, didn't have to get anxious about a long drive or a poor weather forecast. For the first time in a month, we had true freedom and it felt like the world had finally been eased off my shoulders.

I glanced over at Pedro, reclining in his seat, arms spread, legs up on the chair in front of him. It had been a long 30 days but they've come to an end. Tomorrow morning he's catching a flight back to Philly and he'll be able to see Krystal.

I look down at Joey who gazes out over the field, also reclined and basking in the rays of satisfaction. His eyes have opened much wider since we started and he has seen how much there really is out there. I wonder how much longer he'll remain in his little studio above the cheesesteak shop…

I look at my dad and my brother. They knew how important this moment was for me and they traveled all the way from Philadelphia to share it with me, displaying their usual amount of support. It means the world to me to see them here. And I think of my mom, who booked us the hotel before we left knowing all along that we'd make it.

Carrie sits next to me and I look at her. I'm 25 and we've been friends our entire lives and we've been through a lot together. Despite the physical distance now between us, our lives are forever intertwined and our minds always connected. Growing up, we spent every day together and I think that's the reason why we think alike. I would not be the person I am today if not for her.

I glance over at Tom, his sunglasses on, watching the game. If not for him, we would not be here. 30in30 would be just another idea in my head. He gave us the adventure of a lifetime and he gave it to us without any expectations. His faith and his courage is inspiring and if that's not a friend, then I don't know what is.

I sipped my Stella. That's delicious… so good on a summer day. Just to my right, I watch a dad high-five his little son after he successfully finished his own rendition of 'Take Me Out To the Ballgame' during the 7th Inning Stretch.

3:30pm

After the game in which the Friars beat the Reds 3-1 on the back of a Jake Peavy complete game, we hung out on the hill in the public park in center. Bring some lawn chairs or some picnic blankets and setup camp out here – this is the place to be during a Pads game.

"You bring a glove?" my dad asks me.

"Of course I brought I glove," I told him.

"This is the perfect place for a catch," he said reaching into his backpack. I reached into my bag and pulled out that glove with 'T.S.G.' written in thick marker. He noticed it immediately and smiled when he realized that its been by my side the whole time. I pounded my fist in its deep pocket for him to throw the ball and he fired one at me. A loud *thump!* and a burst of that sweet rawhide scent filled the air around me.

What a perfect day.

"So you doing it again next summer?" my dad asked.

I thought about it for a minute. "Nah, I don't think so. I think next year might be minor league parks."

And I threw the old, weathered baseball back to my dad.

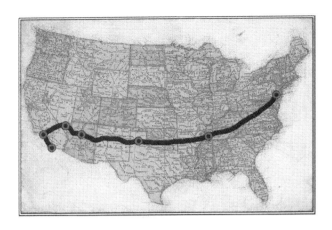

Epilogue

We let loose that night – all of us – and having my close friends and family there made it all the more special. We had nowhere to drive tonight and nowhere to be tomorrow and that was just fine by us.

Pedro caught his flight home early the next morning, Carrie drove back for classes, and my dad and Wes left early that afternoon. Joey and I were alone in the room with SportsCenter on the TV and a beer in our hands.

"What are you doing today?" I asked Joey.

"Nuthin. You?"

I shrugged my shoulders. "I dunno. I was thinking about maybe going back up to LA for another night." It felt weird not having anything to do, not having an agenda for the day, not having a deadline to meet.

We have seven days to get the Vanbino back to the rental office in Philly so the drive home will be a leisurely one. Finally, we can take our time.

"Sounds good to me," Joey agreed.

*　　　*　　　*

From LA, we'd skip over to Vegas and spend a night there, then from Vegas head over to the Grand Canyon. We drove through the juniper tree forest in the desert and through herds of wild steer before winding up at a tiny bed and breakfast on Route 66 in Williams, Arizona.

We went to a little bar that night and got to talking to the bartender. She was probably in her 50's I'd say, filling out the crossword puzzle in her paper on this slow night. There were two others there, locals no doubt, because they all knew each other by name.

"I've been doing a lot of thinking lately, ya know? I hate home. And this trip has done nothing but open my eyes to how much there is out there," Joey disclosed to his new bartender friend.

"Where's home?"

"Philly now but I grew up in a little town right outside the Poconos."

"The Poconos!? Oh my God, I love it out there. Some of the most beautiful scenery I've ever seen... and I've been all over." She takes a puff on her cigarette. "The

Poconos. My gosh." She looks at Joey nodding her head, smiling in approval.

"It's pretty I guess but I dunno... it's not Laguna Beach or San Diego."

"Let me tell you something – I grew up right here, right here and I hated it. Hated everything about it." She spoke in a raspy voice, a burning cigarette between her fingers that leaves a trail of smoke in the air as her hands moved when she talked. "And I traveled everywhere – everywhere – but it wasn't until I left that I could truly appreciate the beauty that I had here. I had been looking for something that happened to be right in front of my eyes the whole time. You don't miss it till it's gone... that's true."

*　　　*　　　*

Past Albuquerque, we found a little restaurant called Rosie's right next to a Little League ball field that had no grass – just course sand and jagged, little rocks.

"I guess this is what baseball is like in the desert," I said standing on the crooked pitching rubber that was just a piece of weathered 2x4. Other than the restaurant and the ball field, there was nothing else around for as far as the eye could see. We ate in Rosie's – I had the best meatloaf I ever had in my life and Joey had the best bacon cheeseburger he's ever had in his life. His cheeseburger was as big as his head and we really broke the bank here – $15 for the lunches and two Coronas.

*　　　*　　　*

A little further ways east down I-40 in Texas, I noticed billboards daring us to take a 72oz. Steak Challenge at a steakhouse in Amarillo. How could we pass this up? I know I said I'm going to eat better but c'mon! I can't pass *this* up! We made it to the Big Texan and before I knew it, I found myself up on a stage in front of the entire restaurant. The Challenge – finish a 72oz. sirloin, a baked potato, a salad, three fried shrimp and a roll in under an hour and get the meal free and my name forever engraved on their Wall of Fame.

I failed. I had to pay $72. But I gave it a good go – I got over halfway through the steak, which isn't bad I guess for a 175lb. guy. And to be honest, I didn't stop because I was full, I stopped because my jaw hurt from chewing so much. I had people cheering for me, though, and these really nice old ladies from Mississippi who were traveling in a church group started coming up in herds to slip one's and five's in my hand. We ended up making $45! They said I reminded them of Joel Osteen. Thank you church group from Mississippi.

The 72oz. steak was one giant piece of meat and I was curious what part of the cow such a huge cut could have come from. So, before the leaving the Big Texan, I asked the waiter.

"Where do you think?" he said with a smirk.

"The ass?" I asked.

He smiled, winked and walked away.

From there, we cut through Oklahoma and Arkansas to Memphis where we stayed for a night on Beale Street and visited Graceland and Sun Studios the following day.

"There's no way I'm driving 20,000 miles across the country and not stopping to see the King," Joey, the Elvis fanatic, said.

After touring Graceland, Joey is now convinced Elvis is still alive.

"Think about it, man. Graceland is a money trap! He's making more money now than he ever did when he was alive... it's genius! Look at all these people! He's living a quiet life on a beach somewhere. Guaranteed."

He had a point and, to be honest, I agree with him.

"You know, I could probably eat one of these sandwiches every day for the rest of my life," I said as I ate a grilled peanut butter and banana sandwich.

After Graceland, we stopped by the famous Sun Studios right down the street. "Pedro would have loved this," I thought. "He's a huge Johnny Cash fan."

And then from Sun Studios it was straight on to Philly, 16 hours away.

*   *   *

I woke up and through groggy eyes I could see Citizens Bank Park off in the distance.

"Is that the ballpark over there?" I asked, still finding my bearings.

"That's the ballpark! Where it all started!!" We turned onto Broad Street and then onto Passyunk in South Philly and drove through Joey's neighborhood.

Joey looks around and names the places with fondness as if he hasn't been down this road in years. "There's my grocery store, my Dunkin' Donuts... my local bar... it's like I never left." I look at him and I can see that he is smiling as he sees the familiar strip again like an old man returning to the neighborhood where he grew up.

We park outside the cheesesteak place that Joey's apartment sits on top of and I help him carry his stuff upstairs. Joey opens his front door.

"Ohhh, nice and toasty in here," he says walking in. He drops his bag and stands in the middle of his small, studio apartment, hands on hips, looking around. He's having a moment and I don't interrupt.

"I hate this apartment but it feels so good. It's weird." He walks around and looks at a Mike Schmidt autographed ball that sits on a shelf. Picks it up and examines it closer. "You know all those places, the Tampa's, the Laguna Beaches, the LA's... all those places are so nice and great to visit but they're not home, you know?" He puts the Mike Schmidt ball back in its place. Then, mostly to himself, he says softly, "they're not home."

Then he walks to his bed and collapses.

"Alright, man. I'll see ya tomorrow." I give him a fist pump and walk out.

I sit in the Vanbino, completely alone for the first time in 36 days. What a weird, almost surreal feeling to be alone in the Vanbino...

I think about how happy Joey was as he walked into his little studio apartment above the cheesesteak shop in South Philly for the first time in over a month. The whole Trip, especially when we were in places like Miami and San Diego, he kept saying how much he hates it where he lives, how he has to think some things over, how he has to move... but as I watched him crash onto *his* bed, in *his* apartment, in *his* neighborhood, I realized, as did he, that he loves it here.

T.S. Eliot said:

And the end of all our exploring,
Will be to arrive where we started,
And know the place for the first time.

Joey's had his paradise all along but it took an epic journey for him to rediscover it.

*   *   *

The next day, Joey and I drove over the bridge to Jersey so my family could help us clean out the Vanbino before returning it to Hertz. Yes – it was so bad we needed an entire cleaning crew. It was littered with crumpled up fast food wrappers, empty bottles and cups of Coke and coffee, and the carpet was coated with a layer of spit-out sunflower seed shells. Two hours and several trash bags later, she was sparkling.

We're on our way to Hertz now and I hate to admit it, but I'm actually going to be a little emotional dropping her off. She was the fourth member of our Team, she didn't give us one problem along the way, and we came to know her just as well as we came to know each other. We couldn't have done it without her.

When we picked her up a month ago, she had 12,000 miles under her wheels and now her odometer reads just over 30,000. I wonder what kind of reaction we'll get from the guy checking us in...

Good thing we got unlimited miles.

BY THE NUMBERS

Baseball fans love their stats. So here's some for you –

Total Miles – Over 18,000
Hours on the Road – 334 give or take (just under 14 full
                                        days)
Oil Changes – 3
Flat Tires – 0
Times the Vanbino was Cleaned – 3
Days the Vanbino Smelled Like Shit – 30
Bottles of Febreze – 4
Times Pulled Over – 3
Speeding Tickets – 2 (both Pedro… I told you he has the
                                        lead foot)
Parking Tickets – 1
Times Getting Lost – 2

Total Time of Baseball Watched – 83 hours, 15 minutes
Runs Scored – 294
Pitches – 8,371
Hits – 497
HR's – 49
Grand Slams – 3
Errors – 44
Rain Delays – 3
Home Team Record – 20-10

Hotdogs – 90-110 (between the 3 of us)
Beers – Impossible to say
McDonald's Iced Coffees – 24 (between Joey and I)
Bags of Sunflower Seeds – 21
Bags of Jerky – 16
Times Throwing-Up – 2 (both Joey)
Weight Gained – 36 lbs. (between the 3 of us)
Times Attempted to Get On Fan-O-Vision – Countless

Times On Fan-O-Vision – 0

Total Cost – Between gas, food, tickets, and hotels, we spent
between $15-$20,000. (Should have kept the
receipts…)

For pictures, videos and movie information, visit our website at 30ballparks30days.com.

17914091R20133

Made in the USA
Charleston, SC
07 March 2013